Forty Miles of Bad Road ✪ *Stars Campaign for Interracial Friendship*
& the 1958 Notting Hill Riots

Forty Miles of Bad Road

Stars Campaign for Interracial Friendship
& the 1958 Notting Hill Riots

by
Rick Blackman

a Redwords book

REDWORDS

Forty Miles of Bad Road: Stars Campaign for Interracial Friendship & the 1958 Notting Hill Riots
Published by Redwords 2017
ISBN: 978-1910-885-536
Design and production: Roger Huddle
Redwords is linked to Bookmarks: the Socialist Bookshop
1 Bloomsbury Street London WC1B 3QE
    redwords.org.uk
    bookmarksbookshop.co.uk

About the author: Rick Blackman is a lecturer in Modern History at Liverpool Hope University and is currently researching a PhD in Music and Anti-Fascism in Post-WWII Britain. He is a musician, songwriter, arranger and producer and is currently involved in a wide variety of musical projects. He is also a trade unionist, socialist and anti-racist activist. He has no spare time.

Contents

Acknowledgements

I WOULD LIKE to thank Dr Mike Brocken for all his help in this work. I am especially grateful to founding SCIF members Hylda Sims, Karl Dallas, Dame Cleo Laine, Rosemary Squires and Marty Wilde for their time in answering my questions and sharing their memories with me. Dr Marika Sherwood was very helpful in reference to material relating to Claudia Jones. Thanks to Christian Høgsbjerg and Sally Campbell for help and advice. Cheers to Billy Bragg, Tony Higgins, Mitch Mitchell and Jason Brummell for compiling their top tens. I would also like to thank Cathy Cross.

Rick Blackman April 2017

Cleo Laine and John Dankworth

Foreword

'Britain was not the multicultural place that it is today in 2017, and many of the things we now take for granted were not there in 1958. After the events in Notting Hill that summer we felt that we had to do something, we had to respond to the violence and the racism that had caused the riots. The best way we knew how was through music. My late husband John Dankworth and I were proud of the part we played in SCIF and our attempt to make England a more tolerant society.'

Dame Cleo Laine, founding SCIF member

'In the fifties black music, was becoming more and more influential in British culture through the increasing availability of recorded American music; through jazz, rock n roll, skiffle, calypso and blues along with visits of various black artists - Muddy Waters, Big Bill Broonzy, Harry Belafonte and more - to this country. It inspired the 'do it yourself' music, the democratisation of performance, which has become the foundation of almost all popular music since that time.

The age of the teenager was with us then - independent, money in the pocket, restless, loving the beat, loving the jive, providing the screaming, bopping audience for this relatively new phenomenon when not attempting to play and sing the stuff themselves.

It was therefore shocking when some of that same rocking n rolling generation, perhaps under the influence of racists like Colin Jordan, took to the streets of Notting Hill and Nottingham to beat up and even kill their black and brown neighbours and contemporaries.

Ignorance, frustration, envy, had a lot to do with it we felt. A different example needed to be set. Stars Campaign for Interracial Friendship, as the name suggests, sought to convert rather than condemn these teenage marauders by example. It sought to show that the stars of TV, screen and radio that they so admired, were not in any way supportive of their behaviour, that it was deplorable, ignorant and a threat to the very culture they espoused. I am proud to have been a small part of that first, short-lived musical campaign against race hatred, together with my skiffle group The City Ramblers.'

Hylda Sims, founding SCIF member

'I am proud to have supported what was a very worthwhile anti-racist project'

Rosemary Squires, SCIF member

01: High Hopes

At the time of writing, 2017, headlines in the British newspapers have returned to familiar, worrying territory. Apocalyptic visions of a lost British civilisation and a disappearing 'Englishness' surround us and were consistently evoked in the run-up to the EU referendum. Politicians and the popular media are once again referring to those fleeing war, or simply seeking to improve their lives, as 'swarms', 'invaders' and 'marauding hordes'. The political far-right has split from its diminutive size into smaller uncontrollable factions that capitalise on every sensationalised media story about crime or alleged increases in immigration. Demonstrations against Islam and random attacks on black, Asian and eastern European people appear with increased frequency. Recently we have seen a growth in anti-Semitism and the desecration of Jewish graves. The Brexit result comes after a twenty year high-profile campaign, antagonistic toward the free movement of labour inside Europe. Much of this has come from the right of centre euro-sceptic wing of the Conservative party. Hostile to the European Union, as they were to the Common Market before it, they and their allies in the media, and indeed some on the right of the Labour party, have presented a narrative of unemployment, erosion of wage levels, a housing crisis and social tensions created by the influx of foreign labour. In the last ten years this hostility has been given succour by a new development in British politics, the United Kingdom Independence Party (UKIP), a populist right wing party openly opposed to immigration into the UK and the whole European political project. On the continent fascist and far-right parties have flourished, thriving on anti-immigration platforms, for example, Jobbik in Hungary, the Front National in France, the Swedish Democrats and Golden Dawn in Greece. An echo of this is found in the election of Donald Trump in the US.

Much of this we have seen before, in Europe and here in the UK. As early as 1919 Conservative Member of Parliament Ernest Wilde demanded that Germans residing in England after WWI should be required to wear a badge at all times demonstrating their ethnic and national origin. In the 1930s there was the rise of antisemitism and Mosley's Blackshirts. By the mid 1970s we witnessed an enormous surge in support for the fascist National Front (NF). The rise of the NF was based solely on a racist repatriation programme, directed at Africans, Afro-Caribbeans and Asians. In the 1980s and 1990s the British National Party (BNP) grew from the ashes of the NF and took centre stage as it launched its interpretation of a fascist programme, again racially motivated. Throughout British history there have been periods where an antipathy toward 'foreigners' has swelled into political movements. There has, however, always been resistance to such xenophobic and racist ideas. The opposition to this discrimination manifests itself in a wide variety of ways: the self-organisation of the ethnic groups directly affected, community groups, legal recourse, political organisations such as Stand Up To Racism and Hope Not Hate; and a tradition of physical opposition to racism and fascism from the Communist Party in the 1930s, to the Anti-Nazi League in the 1970s and now organisations such as Unite Against Fascism and Anti-Fascist Network.

Alongside these political routes in opposing racism there has always been an artistic interpretation of fighting oppression from around the world. Nova Cançó in Spain under Franco, Tropicalismo in Brazil in the 1960s. Even in Nazi Germany there were underground jazz clubs where attendance could mean the concentration camp if detected (see Appendix iii). In the UK the Theatre Workshop and the Workers Music Association under the auspices of Joan Littlewood and Ewan MacColl respectively, pushed progressive and political art to working class people in the years after WWII. In the late 1970s Rock Against

Racism used punk rock and reggae to organise against the far right. So whenever racist or fascist ideas appear we have seen an artistic response.

In the late 1950s, in the aftermath of the Notting Hill riots, a home grown anti-racist, anti-fascist organisation was born that attempted such a cultural opposition to racism: the Stars Campaign for Interracial Friendship (SCIF). SCIF used music to undermine the racism of the far right and this is their story. For this book I have undertaken research using a variety of tools: archive resources from local libraries, national newspapers, historical documents from the British Library, footage available on the internet; and interviews with the few who were active in SCIF at the time. Two contemporaneous studies were invaluable: *Newcomers, West Indians in London* written by sociologist Ruth Glass in 1960 and *Immigration, Race and Politics* by journalist Paul Foot written in 1965. Each supplied an extensive and comprehensive account of the personal experiences and political expressions of 1950s immigration and both provide a sympathetic understanding of it. No such careful research or empiricism exists from those opposed to immigration.

For almost sixty years SCIF has been lost to history. Much of what I have found, therefore, means I am the first to discuss its existence academically and there is no political discourse available. Hopefully this will now change and discussion and alternate interpretation may arise. During the short time SCIF existed, the most significant political organisation on the left (outside of the Labour Party) was the Communist Party of Great Britain (CP). Whilst resolutely opposed to the racism and fascism of the 1950s as it had been to the fascism and anti-Semitism of the 1930s, little historical analysis exists from the CP or historians of the party on this particular part of British history.

As far as possible I have tried to remain objective, however when your subject matter involves violent attacks on black people and even murder by organisations openly supporting Hitler, I may sometimes have drifted toward subjectivity.

No art is separate from the society that it exists in, so a musical response to a political phenomenon requires both a musical and a political analysis. In order to understand the period discussed in this work it has been unavoidable that I look to history to explain how events developed and escalated during 1958 and 1959. Therefore, it has been essential that I include a brief history of British fascism, how it operated in the 1930s and 1940s and how it used the lessons it learnt from these decades in order to try to be a more efficient force in the 1950s. That British fascism was ultimately unsuccessful does not negate its inclusion here, rather I believe it is unlikely that one could analyse the period without it.

For similar reasons an attempt at understanding the plight faced by Afro-Caribbeans – their housing, employment opportunities and general standard of living – was also needed. Without it, the strategy and tactics adopted by SCIF would be incomprehensible. Placing events in their historical context is crucial for any historian. Understanding the steps taken by SCIF to oppose discrimination without transposing them into our present day society is vital. The strategy and tactics adopted to counteract the prejudice suffered by black people in the 1950s has to be seen from their and not our perspective. They had not the fifty-nine years of organisation, legislation and demonstrations against racism that we, in 2017, have. There was no British anti-racist history in any real sense to learn from in 1958, and here was my major stumbling block. In my research I was looking for events that simply did not happen in the 1950s. True, there had been mass meetings and demonstrations peppered throughout British history: the Chartists, the Suffragettes, the Great Unrest and the General Strike for example, but the type of demonstrations against racism or the anti-apartheid rallies of the 1970s onwards were not possible in 1958 as a movement had not gathered enough political momentum or reached the critical mass necessary to enact such huge undertakings. So I spent much time looking for something that physically and politically did not exist.

Likewise, as SCIF was a musical endeavour, I searched for grandiose concerts and raucous gigs where audiences of tens of thousands applauded the music and radical political sentiments of the artists. Once again it was the historical setting and the music technology that was available in the late 1950s that dictated what type of concerts were possible, not my sub-conscious yearnings. Although dance halls and live music existed, and there were jazz and blues festivals up and running by 1958, these were largely acoustic affairs. Local gigs were usually in youth clubs, the back rooms of pubs and – for the really successful groups – dank basements in Soho. If these groups had amplifiers at all, the two guitars and the vocals would be plugged into one tiny 18 Watt amp. The rhythm section suffered the most. Bassists 'played' a tea chest bass, which was an upside down wooden tea chest, a broomstick and a piece of string suitably attached. Drums, such as they were, consisted of a washboard, a few thimbles and a lot of enthusiasm. Even the introduction of the electric guitar would prove challenging to some and stories of electrocution were not uncommon as those new to guitar playing would plug one end of their lead into their freshly purchased 'electric' guitar, change the jack plug on the other end to a mains plug and then proceed to insert it in a socket! Mass consumption of recorded and amplified music outdoors in the 1950s was most often enjoyed at fairgrounds. Even ten years later than the period we are discussing here, the PA used by the Rolling Stones at the 1969 free Hyde Park gig (a Watkins 1500 watt) is comical by modern day standards (the PA used at Glastonbury 2016 was 100,000 watts). Consequently, I could not find massive SCIF gigs in 1958 or 1959, not because they didn't happen, but because they couldn't happen. The technology was simply not there.

Culturally, they lived in a world where not only was the television in black and white, but so was society. Multi-coloured TV was ten years away, multiculturalism even further. A concert such as Nelson Mandela's 70th birthday celebration in June 1988 at Wembley stadium would have been inconceivable in 1959 for both political and music technology reasons. The activities SCIF undertook therefore, were small scale, but only in comparison to later events in the 1970s and onwards. Black and white people were simply not allowed to convene in the same establishment in the late 1950s, so to set up multi-racial dances, when none, literally none, existed, minutes from the headquarters of a violent white supremacist organisation was not only courageous, but one of the few tools available to artists at the time.

This is not to say that Britain employed a racial system such as Apartheid in South Africa or Jim Crow in the southern states of America, ours was a more insidious modus-operandi. The so-called colour bar was everywhere, not always visible as it was in housing, but often with a more deleterious effect in a work or a social setting. Consequently, racism presented itself in ways that were not always obvious. Combatting this prejudice required dexterity. Many from SCIF had no experience in such terrain and had no reference points to cite, others had vast experience in labour struggles and fighting oppression, but outside of England. Either way, this was new territory and in many ways they were writing the guidebook for what was to follow.

02: London is the Place for Me

Britain has always been a
multi-racial society. Sometimes seen and sometimes hidden. Since
Roman times there has been an African presence. As the possessor
of the largest empire in history, a slave trader par excellence and
with London for centuries the financial capital of the world, the
movement and exchange of cultures and peoples was inevitable. For
500 years there has been a black community in London, in the 1850s
Liverpool housed the biggest Chinese community outside of China,
Bristol has records of a slave or freed slave enclave for some 400 years,
and following the arrival of the East India Company to the Indian
sub-continent there has been an Asian presence in the UK since
the early 17th century. As Britain impacted upon the world, so the
world affected change on it. Revolutionary upheavals in Europe, the
collapse of rival empires and war all contributed to the ever-changing
ingredients that became modern Britain.

The end of the Second World War saw dramatic changes to British
society. Although the national government, and especially Winston
Churchills' rhetoric throughout the conflict had been to rid the
world of fascism and to fight for freedom and democracy, the post-
war reality was different. Britain's indifference to fascist Spain and
Portugal and the bombing of partisans to enable the re-installation
of collaborators and known fascists in Greece gave the lie to the war's
declared aims. The Yalta and Potsdam conferences carved up the map
of Europe into spheres of political and economic influence between
the victors. Britain's attitude to empire also ran contrary to its
grand statements of liberty for all, with one exception. The fight for

independence that had escalated under Gandhi's tutelage and the sub-continent's enormous sacrifice during the war had left India pregnant with political expectation.[1] The jewel in the crown was to demand self-determination, and demand it very quickly. India and Pakistan won independence in 1947. However, this was not the case elsewhere in the British Empire. Although many colonies had burgeoning national liberation movements, no other country would see itself free from British rule for some twelve years.[2] Continued colonial rule was in contradiction to the Atlantic Charter, the agreement between Great Britain and the USA that was to be the blueprint for post WWII independence and stated that 'all peoples have a right to self-determination'.

The war had left large parts of Britain in ruins; the rebuilding of cities at its end would necessitate a high demand for labour. Initially soldiers were requisitioned and prisoners of war were used as labourers to help this process. Also there were over 120,000 Poles who had stayed in England at the war's end.[3] This pool of labour was to prove insufficient and the government had to look further afield for fresh supplies. On 22 June 1948 the Empire Windrush docked from Jamaica and a new chapter in British society began. The small existing black populations in London, Liverpool and Bristol would not only grow, but this first influx of 492 Jamaicans was the beginning of a real and permanent change in British society.[4] Many of the men who arrived on Windrush had been stationed in England during the war. Indeed tens of thousands of Africans, Afro-Americans, West Indians and Asians had spent the conflict's duration living in the UK helping with the war effort.[5] In 1948 the Labour government passed the Nationality Act which granted United Kingdom citizenship to all people from the colonies and ex-colonies. British passports were issued and the right to come and live in Britain was granted for life. Although at first the flow was slow, Caribbean migration began to increase in the following years:

> In October 1948, the Orbita brought 180 into Liverpool, and three months later, 39 Jamaicans, 15 of them women, arrived in Liverpool...next summer, the Georgic brought 253 West Indians, 45 of them women. A few hundred came in 1950, about 1,000

in 1951, about 2,000 in 1952 and again in 1953. Larger numbers arrived in the next four years, including many wives and children of men who had settled here: 24,000 in 1954; 26,000 in 1956; 22,000 in 1957; 16,000 in 1958. Ten years after the Empire Windrush there were in Britain about 125,000 West Indians who had come over since the end of the war.[6]

During this time an active recruitment process had been initiated from the UK for industrial labour, for example, London Transport had by April 1956 sent several representatives to Barbados offering not just careers, but loans to pay for passage to England. These loans were to be deducted from wages after people had started work as bus drivers and conductors. This process would continue into the 1960s expanding into Trinidad and Jamaica. The British Hotels and Restaurants Association also recruited from the West Indies and Conservative Minister for Health Enoch Powell sought Caribbean workers to clean the hospital corridors and nurse in the hospital wards of the newly founded National Health Service. Alongside this, similar recruitment had begun in the Indian sub-continent – by 1958 around 55,000 Indians and Pakistanis had arrived in Britain.[7]

Historically many West Indians had seen emigration to the USA as a pre-war economic solution to their financial woes. America was the world's most powerful economy, it had jobs, it had opportunity. It also had the music and the clothes that were so popular and influential to the development of indigenous Caribbean culture in both the pre- and post-war years.[8] Although as subjects of the Queen many Afro-Caribbeans considered England the 'mother country', America was the greater attraction. However, this main thrust of pre-war migration was to change. Four things contributed: firstly, the positive experience during WWII of thousands of young West Indian men and women who had gone to Britain to assist in the war effort. Secondly, Britain's drive for labour to fuel their post-war economic boom. Thirdly the 1948 Nationality Act which gave British citizenship for life to all colonial subjects and lastly the McCarran-Walker Act of 1952 that restricted Caribbean entry into America.

Upon arrival, irrespective of their experience, qualifications and what

employment they had been promised, many of the jobs that black
people were offered were menial and unskilled. As Fryer explains:

> Most white people in this country believed – and many still suppose
> – that the bulk of them [West Indians] were unskilled manual
> workers. But that is not so. Of the men who came here, a mere 13
> percent had no skills, of the women only 5 percent. In fact, one in
> four of the men and half of the women were non manual workers,
> and almost half the men (46 percent) and over a quarter of the
> women (27 percent) were skilled manual workers.[9]

So, many of these young men and women were employed in
occupations they were overqualified to do, moreover their
remuneration for this labour did not have parity with their
white co-workers. This though, was only the beginning of their
disappointment. They received a less than welcoming reception
from their workmates. Many white workers were opposed to the
employment of black workers at all, white was promoted over black
irrespective of experience or qualification and demands for quotas
to keep black labour to a minimum rang out from the factory floors.
The usual recourse to justice for the working class, the trade union
movement, was also a hostile environment for black labour. Let us
look briefly at the environment that greeted the new arrivals in one
industry, on the buses:

> In 1955 Wolverhampton bus drivers banned overtime 'as a protest
> against the increasing numbers of coloured workers employed'. The
> Transport and General Workers Union insisted that no more than
> 52 of the city's 900 bus workers should be black. A branch secretary
> said they were not operating a colour bar, but 'don't intend to have
> platform staff made up to its full strength by coloured people only.'
> West Bromwich bus workers staged one-day strikes in 1955 against
> the employment of a solitary Indian conductor, and a TGWU official
> said: 'I do not think there is any racial antagonism behind this'. The
> Bristol Omnibus Company refused to take on black crews until a
> boycott of its buses by black people forced a change of policy.[10]

The craft unions fared no better, as one black clerical worker
sardonically explained: Union: 'Get a job and we will give you

membership.' Employer: 'Join the union and we will get you a job'.[11] Although the General Council to the Trades Union Congress had a policy that denounced discrimination, at local branch level:

> There was a gap, sometimes a wide one, between policy at top level and the attitudes at other levels. While the 'high command' of a trade union passes resolutions deploring colour prejudice, the local branches may operate colour quotas.[12]

When and if the day's work was done, a place to rest your head was to prove even more difficult.

No Blacks, No Dogs, No Irish

The level of open hostility to the new immigrants fitted into a prejudice that had been honed over decades. The Huguenots, German émigrés and Jews had all suffered. The Irish, Britain's first casualty of empire, had been systematically discriminated against for centuries; the skin colour this time was different but the practices remained the same. With the enormous mobilisation of African-American, African, West Indian and Asian troops stationed in Britain for the war's duration, it would be reasonable to expect a certain familiarity of the British with other races within living memory. However, the opposite appears to be true. According to Fryer half the British population had never met a black person and those that had had not formed any lasting friendships. Over 66% held a 'low opinion' of black people and of those half again were malevolent.[13] Confines of space do not allow a full discussion of the reasons for this racism, suffice to say that centuries of empire; the ideological justification for imperialism and the inhumane treatment of black people in the slave system that preceded it had permeated its poison into every corner of British society.

Socially, a 'colour bar' was in operation all over the country. What this meant in reality was not just discrimination in employment and housing but a duplicitous inequity in restaurants, hotels, dance halls, bars and pubs. Sometimes an open refusal into establishments would be in operation, commonly there would be signs prohibiting entrance to 'coloured people'. If they did make it into a pub to buy a drink and were unmolested, black people could stand at a bar, be ignored for the whole evening and not served.

Slum housing was often the only option available to the new arrivals. Countless testaments of black people regale the tale of arriving at a property that they had been assured was available, only to be informed that it had been let when the colour of their skin became apparent. However, the living conditions of working class white families were not of a superior nature. Indeed, the area that most concerns us in this work, North Kensington, was notorious for some of the worst housing in the capital. Portland Road – one of the main thoroughfares that runs through the district – was classified as unfit for human habitation as early as 1886 when social reformer Charles Booth created his colour coded poverty map of the capital. He used the colour yellow to describe the middle to upper class and wealthy and the colour black for the lowest class which he called 'vicious and semi-criminal'.[14] He concluded:

> ... the area to the west was black: as deep and dark a type as anywhere in London...[inhabited by] the lowest class which consists of some occasional labourers, street sellers, loafers, criminals and semi-criminals. Their life is the life of savages, with vicissitudes of extreme hardship and their only luxury is drink.[15]

Today as then, one end of Portland Place remains firmly yellow and the other black.[16] Post-war tenants were bullied, exploited and harassed by ruthless landlords, though there was some protection afforded them by legislation. This all changed with the passing of the Rent Act in 1957. Prime Minister Harold Macmillan's Conservative government removed the statutory restrictions on the rents of privately let accommodation which had been operative since the First World War. The government argued that by abolishing rent controls landlords would be encouraged to maintain, improve and invest in private rented property and thereby increase its availability and standard. In reality what the 1957 Act did was to enable unscrupulous and racketeering landlords like the notorious Peter Rachman to run amok in the area. At liberty to now charge whatever rent he wanted, in whatever squalid conditions, Rachman proceeded to evict (often with menaces) the existing white tenants from their homes and install the recent émigrés from the West Indies in their place. Now with no statutory protection from the law and often unable to secure rented property elsewhere, the black community was given little choice but to accept the exorbitant and rat infested slums offered by Rachman and his like. For many in the already prejudiced white community, convinced 'their' jobs were being taken away, the eviction tactic adopted by Rachman and others was further fuel on the fire. Now, so they thought, their homes were not safe either. It was these small flames that the groups of fascists around Oswald Mosley and Colin Jordan were to fan in 1958 and 1959.

Notes

1   India had provided the largest volunteer army in history, the British Indian Army, some 2.5 million strong. Also they had suffered the Bengal famine which killed around the same number in 1943. McKenzie (1951) p1.

2   Notably Ghana on the 6th March 1957. The fate of Sudan achieving independence one year earlier was inextricably intertwined with the history of Egypt, formally independent in 1922 and politically in 1956. Jamaica and Trinidad became independent in 1962, Guyana and Barbados in 1966, the other Caribbean islands had to wait until the 1970s or 1980s. There are still six Caribbean islands controlled by Britain today.

3   Foot (1965) p117.

4   Fryer (2010) p373.

5   At one point over 100,000 black Americans were in the UK, plus the estimated 8,000 West Indian troops. (Fryer p358, and p362) The experience of the African-American troops was markedly different to the Jim Crow, de-facto segregation, violence and outright racism they had grown up with in the States. Many testaments from black GI'S confirm that there was little or no prejudice exhibited toward them (Fryer p359).

6   Fryer, (2010) p373.

7   Ibid.

8   Jump & Jive and R&B with their rhythmic off beats floated across the airwaves from the southern states into the West Indies and were crucial to the beginning of Ska, Rocksteady and subsequently Reggae. Also the oil drums that enabled that uniquely Trinidadian sound, the steel band, were left by American Navy at the wars end on the island.

9   Fryer (2010) p374.

10   Ibid p376.

11   Ibid.

12   Glass (1960) p76.

13   Fryer (2010) p375.

14   http://booth.lse.ac.uk/static/a/4.html

15   Ibid.

16   According to the *Daily Mail* on 26/05/12, number 22 Portland Road, a five-bedroom semi with a Bulthaup kitchen (whatever that is) and a private cinema, sold for £6m. At the other end of the road, Flat 14 at Winterbourne House fetched a more modest £244,000.

03: Rock with the Caveman

POLITICAL GROUPS in England espousing extreme right wing views can be traced back to late Victorian and Edwardian society with groups like the British Brothers League and the Immigration Reform Association. But British fascism, or a proto-fascism, emerged from the devastation of World War One in its first guise The Britons Society, a nationalist, anti-immigration and fiercely anti-Semitic organisation. Formed in 1918 they began the dissemination of their ideas through a publishing house that continued its operations as the Britons Publishing Society up until the 1970s.[1] By 1923, another far right group, British Fascisti (BF), had emerged. The BF was the first UK party to openly call themselves fascist and although modelling the organisation on Mussolini's National Fascist Party, the BF owed more – both politically and sartorially – to founder Rotha Lintorn Orman's experience as a girl guide in Bournemouth. The BF may have been the first, but they were not alone for long, as other groups of right wing extremists soon operated up and down the country. As we shall see, the history of the British far right is littered with tiny groups, organisations and factions all vying for hegemony and all infected with internecine rivalries that more often than not, combined with the external activities of anti-fascists, precipitate their demise.[2]

Oswald Mosley was elected to parliament at the age of 21 – the youngest MP in the house – in 1922. Initially a member of the Conservative party, he crossed the floor to join the Labour party, then joined the Independent Labour party where he served as a cabinet minister in Ramsay MacDonald's government. Shortly after this he left the ILP to form his own organisation the New Party, which drifted further and further toward the right. After meeting Mussolini in 1932 Mosley fully embraced fascism as a political ideology, folded the New Party and formed the British Union of Fascists (BUF) in October 1932.

Arnold Leese was a veterinary surgeon who had served in India and West Africa, and whose conversion to fascism would overshadow his only other offering to society: *A Treatise on the One-Humped Camel in Health and in Disease*. Leese should always be thus remembered, as the parasite responsible for causing infections in camels' eyes (Thelazia Leesei) is named after him. Joining the British Fascists in 1924, Leese soon became disillusioned with them for not being sufficiently fascist and left. He then proceeded to found the Fascist League (FL) and by 1930 he had become leader of the Imperial Fascist League (IFL). A fanatical anti-Semite, after reading the apocryphal *Protocols of the Elders of Zion*, (which profoundly influenced Hitler), Leese developed a prototype for fascist activity that we will revisit in the 1950s. Leese saw the IFL as a training ground in anti-Semitism and as 'an active organisation for spreading fascist ideas'. This was to be done by IFL 'legions' split into two separate cells, 'active and passive'. The passive were the graduate associations: aristocrats, university alumni and professionals. They disseminated information, wrote the IFL newspaper, *The Fascist*, and produced many pamphlets. They also engaged in fundraising. The active cells were concentrated on the working class, hardened 'street fighters' used as muscle to protect the passive cells and terrorise both the Jewish community and sections of the left. Of course this organisational model was not Leese's own creation; Mussolini had initiated such a tactic in Italy and Hitler had operated along similar lines in the Weimar Republic.

Of the two men organising in London at the time, Mosley was a more savvy political operator than Leese and by 1933 the IFL had been eclipsed by the BUF, much to Leese's chagrin. Thus the headlines for 1930s British fascism are taken by Mosley. Supported by sections of the popular press that fan-fared: 'Hurrah for the Blackshirts' (*The Daily Mail*) and 'Give the Blackshirts a helping hand' (*The Mirror*) newspaper baron Lord Rothermere assisted Mosley in his rise, although the subsequent withdrawal of that support in 1935 was a setback.[3]

> The ending of Rothermere's support and the turn to political anti-Semitism were crucial to the future history of the BUF. Dropped by the one section of the establishment which supported it, and adopting policies that ensured that public opinion would become increasingly hostile, Mosley destroyed whatever small likelihood the BUF had of becoming an effective force in British politics.[4]

Whilst losing establishment support certainly did not help the BUF, this analysis removes the agency of those who organised the opposition to the blackshirts: the constant arguments had with them, the agitation and propaganda about them, and the bravery of those who physically fought against them. Two grandstand events planned in the pre-war decade for Mosley and the BUF both backfired. The first was a mass rally at Olympia in 1934. At this event some 10,000 people attended, however of that 10,000 there were many anti-fascists and the meeting descended into disruption and violence and caused a series of negative reports in the national media which some argue led to the withdrawal of support from Lord Rothermere. The second event, two years later, was to provocatively march through a predominantly Jewish area of east London. Despite massive police presence essentially enabling Mosley's march the BUF did not pass. They were routed. Stopped in their tracks in an area of Whitechapel by a united front of Jews, trade unionists, communists, socialists and local people. The Battle of Cable Street on 4 October 1936, although not the final page in Mosley's political life, nor the story of British fascism, was certainly the end of this particular chapter. With the outbreak of WWII the BUF was proscribed and the ragtag collection of British Nazis were gathered up and interned under Defence Regulation 18b, suspending Habeas Corpus. Many would remain in prison until the war's end.

The 43 Group

The horrors of WWII, the estimated 58 million dead, the Holocaust and Europe left in ruins did nothing to dampen the spirit of the

British far right. Unrepentant, Thurlow estimates that there were some twenty-four different fascist groups of varying shapes and sizes at the war's end.[5] Mosley was released to house arrest in 1943, although unable to undertake any activity until 1945. Only sixteen weeks after VJ day (15 August 1945), Mosley addressed his first post war rally to an audience of 600.[6] Ever the opportunist and political operator Mosley began to slowly rebuild his movement and political profile. No longer calling himself or his organisation fascist, he set about building a new party, the Union Movement (UM).

> Mosley himself had set aside an estimated £400,000 out of his large fortune, plus he anticipated those industrialists and aristocrats who had funded him before the war would do so again. Some 250 wealthy members of The Right Club had stayed intact and underground throughout the war and saw the Blackshirts as their main defence against Jews and Communists.[7]

Whilst the war was raging in Europe, a group of disgruntled Tories, anti-Semites and fascists had formed the semi-clandestine coterie The Right Club whose charming motto was Perish Judah! The group had a dual purpose: a) to exert pressure on the government to sue for peace as swiftly as possible; and b) to consolidate British fascism into a central organisation. A key member was A K Chesterton, one-time editor of BUF newspaper *The Blackshirt* who later went on to co-found the National Front. Another familiar face was Arnold Leese, who despite calls for the extermination of Jews as far back as 1935, was now, post war, a Holocaust denier.[8]

Leese published a journal called *Gothic Ripples*, another virulent anti-Semitic diatribe which contained a regular column called Nigger Notes.[9] It was around these people that the fascists began rebuilding after the war. There were remnants of pre-war anti-Semitism in London and fascist meetings proliferated during the late 1940s. The Israel-Palestine conflict and the stationing and killing of British troops still not returned from WWII fanned these racist flames. Headlines in *The Fascist* cried 'Our boys being murdered by Jewish terrorists in Palestine'.[10] A new wave of far right groups appeared.[11] Hundreds of fascist meetings occurred each month up and down the country, although the epicentre was in London. Constant opposition to these meetings was organised by the 43 Group, a combative Jewish ex-servicemen's and women's organisation that propagandised against the fascists and physically broke up their meetings (estimated by leading 43 Group member Morris Beckman at an average of fifteen per week).[12] Worried at this constant threat and unable to gain purchase in the wider political areas Mosley attempted to coalesce the disparate Nazis into one party. Mosley concocted a six-point plan:

— The smaller fascist cells should be absorbed into larger ones

— These new larger groups would in turn merge, ceasing all rivalry

— Their meetings would all follow the same program 'Britain for the British'

— Book clubs and discussion groups would be welded into a national organisation for education for the upper and middle class.

— All parts of the organisation would be drawn together to emerge as the Union Movement

— A massive publicity campaign would culminate in large rallies at the end of 1947[13]

Mosley's planned mass meetings did not occur until 1948 and then were all disrupted by the 43 Group and proved to be a flop. Fratricidal rivalries inside the fascist parties reappeared, some individuals left and denounced the UM, some drifted away and some defected to Leese's IFL. Despite repeated requests from the Jewish community, the Labour government allowed Mosley to organise his highly provocative meetings. The British Board of Jewish Deputies, whilst opposing Mosley, acquiesced to the government and their opposition was only in the form of words. Without the open defiance from the 43 Group it is possible that Mosley could have built. Counter demonstrations accompanied the UM almost everywhere they went and what support they had garnered from local people waned. By 1950 the fascists again retired into the shadows.

Notes

1   Thurlow (1987) p67. Every fascist group used this publishing house, from the BUF to the NF.

2   During the 1920s these were: The National Fascisti, The New Party, The Imperial Fascist League and others too numerous to detail here, however two figures are worth noting at this point as they will resurface later on: Oswald Mosley from the New Party and Arnold Leese of the Imperial Fascist league.

3   This is open support for Mosley, whether there was assistance behind closed doors is a matter of conjecture. Rothermere however remained an enthusiastic advocate of both Hitler and Mussolini throughout the 1930s, congratulating Hitler on the annexing of Czechoslovakia in 1938.

4   Thurlow (1987) p105.

5   Ibid p234.

6   Ibid.

7   Beckman (1993) p40.

8   Barberis (2000) p183.

9   Leese lived in Notting Hill Gate at 74 Princedale Road, London W11, more of which later.

10   Beckman (1993) p60.

11   For example, The British Peoples Party, The League of Ex-Servicemen and Women, The Union for British Freedom, The Imperial Defence League.

12   Ibid p89.

13   Beckman (1993) pp83-84.

Top: 'Teddy Boys' in Notting Hill 1958. Below: fascist rally Trafalgar Square 1959.

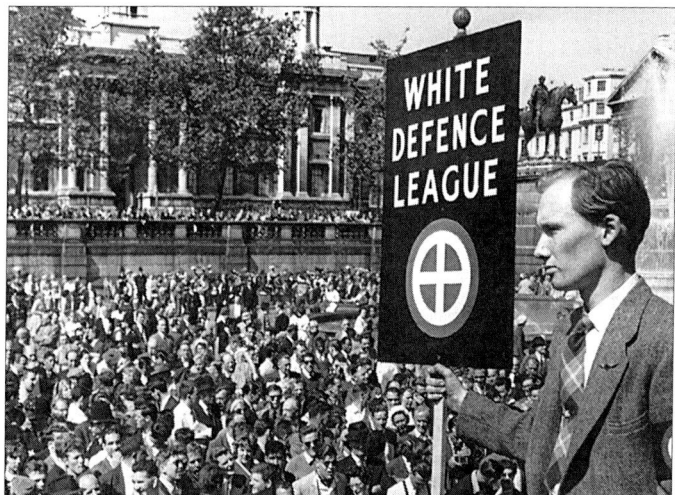

04: On the Street where You Live

FROM 1951 TO 1964 the Conservative party were in government. Immigration ambled on throughout most of the 1950s and the reception to it, on the whole, was lukewarm. By the summer of 1958 the temperature was rising. Opposition to immigration arose in Nottingham and nascent prejudices over job insecurities and interracial relationships erupted into confrontation and two weeks of sustained rioting.[1] Tensions on the streets of west London were also starting to spill over into violence. Throughout July assaults against black people increased. At the end of that month a group of Teddy Boys attacked a black owned café in Askew Road, Shepherds Bush (just a mile west of Notting Hill), seriously injuring the owner and causing £250 worth of damage.[2] Sporadic and violent incidents took place throughout the following month, but on 24 August two separate and vicious attacks occurred, hospitalising several Caribbean men in Shepherds Bush and Notting Hill and resulting in a police chase and the arrest of a group of white men. There had been rioting of a racial, or to be precise, racist nature before in twentieth century British history: anti-German rioting prior to the First World War, anti-black riots in Liverpool and Cardiff in 1919, anti-Semitic riots throughout the 1930s, anti-Italian riots during WWII. There had also been minor disturbances against the newly arrived Caribbean communities in the late 1940s and early 1950s in Camden, Birmingham and Deptford. But the events about to unfold in Notting Hill were different, as the nation's media would focus upon them like no other. Whether there were any genuine grievances and difficulties over incidents that occurred in the area prior to the riots is almost impossible to decipher. The level of invective and unadulterated racism from the locals who voiced concerns and the absence of any objective police reporting make an analysis difficult.[3]

The animosity toward the Caribbean community is clearly demonstrated by countless letters to the editor each week in one of the local newspapers, the *Kensington News*. Many could be used as examples but they are best illustrated by the following, which although lengthy is worth quoting in full:

Sir – It is quite apparent that your correspondent "Red Robins" in your last week's issue of *Kensington News* must live in a very elite part of Kensington when he suggests that white folk should be more patient and tolerant, believe me, we have no option. It is most deplorable that these immigrants are allowed to squeeze into our homes and flats, our authorities turning a blind eye to overcrowding, this being mainly the cause of vice.

First of all, I would like to emphasise I am neither a supporter or sympathiser of Sir Oswald Mosley or the White Defence League. I was full of pity when they arrived, but my pity now goes to the white folk. They have turned the place into a slum. Hot Dogs being sold all through the night in our streets, to satisfy the coloured folk who frequent the drinking dens. These places are open from the early evening to 6am. The activity is intolerable, and we seldom get a decent night's sleep.

They have acquired the most expensive cars, and yet were seeking assistance when they first arrived. These cars are being driven at the most erratic speeds all through the night, they obviously get much amusement with their screeching brakes. The neighbourhood has sadly deteriorated, and yet our rates go up and up. The district is inundated with prostitutes, and we have many brothels in our houses, cars and taxis drawing up all night.

We have no black colour bar, it is a white colour bar and we are slowly being purged out of our homes, by their unseemly behaviour, thus paving the way for more immigrants. This is the most evil part of London, Soho being a comparatively peaceful neighbourhood.

I have nothing against the coloured workers, who are doing an honourable job, but I do complain bitterly of the street corner louts, who almost compel pedestrians to walk on the roads. They are asleep until mid-day, then, keeping the workers awake most of the night, brawling with prostitutes. I am still looking for the words of sympathy for the white residents, who very soon will have to change their lives, by doing night work and sleep by day.[4]

Running the whole gamut of racist emotions and indicative of the comments voiced by many locals at the time, this letter leaves no stone unturned in identifying what the author judges to be the problem in the borough of Kensington post-Windrush. The overwhelming response to any difficulties white locals faced was that immigration was the problem. Perception of 'another' taking what little there was from an indigenous community is usually simmering just beneath the surface of any outbreak of racial violence. The housing in North Kensington, declared unfit for human habitation in 1886, had seen little done to improve it throughout the following decades. WWII bomb damage had exacerbated an already untenable situation and overcrowding in the housing that was available was rife, scarcity of employment was also an issue. Concerns over prostitution and lawlessness appear again and again in letters to the local newspapers at the time. Wherever poverty and social deprivation reside, 'crime and vice' inevitably accompany them. Local councils had been left with the responsibility of dealing with an influx of people without the resources from government to adequately cope. Writing in 1964 journalist Paul Foot observed:

In that crucial decade of commonwealth immigration (1954-1964), the Conservative Government had no policy about meeting them at the port of arrival; no policy about accommodation; no policy about schooling their children.[5]

Furthermore:

Local councils had no estimate from the central government of the numbers coming into their area, no guidance from Health or Education Ministries on the possibilities of different health and sanitation standards or on the difficulties of teaching children who could not speak English. Had every councillor been a humanist of soaring imagination, pledged unequivocally to assist his brothers from abroad, the problems would still have been insurmountable without some assistance or guidance from the centre.[6]

Clearly there were problems, but who was responsible for the situation and how was it to be overcome?

Edwardian Dandies

Ironically another group of 'outsiders' much debated and much derided at the time, were also to be held responsible for the events about to unfold in Notting Hill Gate. Edwardian dandies, or Teddy Boys as they became known, were disproportionately blamed for many of the ills that occurred in British society in the 1950s and have been the focus of the 1958 Notting Hill riots ever since. Such was the entrenchment into common parlance of 'Teds' as a form of abuse, that in denigrating John Osborne and his play *Look Back In Anger*, one literary reviewer dismissed him as an 'Intellectual Teddy Boy'.[7] But who were the Teddy Boys and where did they come from?

No urban street style or sub-culture truly comes from one singular thing, but the origins of the clothing that gave Teddy Boys their name we can pinpoint to one item of men's attire. In sartorial protest to the ration book austerity of post-war London, Savile Row tailors in the late 1940s began experimenting with suits that harked back to more flamboyant times, those of Edward VII's reign 1901-1910. The cut of the cloth was different:

> ... [the] jacket is generously skirted and button-four with a very short lapel and squarely-cut fronts. Jacket pockets are slanted and are offset by narrow trousers (narrow all the way – not pegged topped) and double breasted waistcoat.[8]

Young affluent men, especially army officers, adopted the look and it also became fashionable in and around Oxbridge universities. Introduced to the world in 1950, the Edwardian style – as it became known – evolved, and as it was adopted by working class youth, it was adapted with other styles, notably the hugely popular western television shows of the time. Pre-dating the rock 'n' roll it has ever since been associated with, Teddy Boys existed in fact fully five years before rock 'n' roll arrived in the UK in 1955. This working class expression of a middle class fashion emanated from Elephant and Castle, south east London, an area noted for its deprivation, then as now. Teddy Boys were also influenced in elements of their dress style by the Spiv. Small time criminals that became notorious in WWII, Spivs were later personified in the British consciousness in the form of Private Walker from Dad's Army and George Cole's character in the St Trinians films. Spivs dealt in illicit black market goods that were in short supply because of wartime and post-war rationing. They were flamboyant and ostentatious dressers at a time when the watchwords for fashion were 'make do and mend'.

But along with this sartorial legacy Teds also inherited an association in the public perception with the petty crime spivs were notorious for. Whether there was any foundation to this accusation or not, the whole sub-culture became tainted by it. Ian Hebdige described this relationship, saying their style becae 'a focus for an illicit delinquent identity'.⁹ Teds and criminality became synonymous. Headlines involving coshes, bicycle chains, razors and flick-knives were commonplace. Violence was the predominant factor associated with Teds, as this excerpt from the *Brighton Herald* demonstrates:

> Strong action is expected by both police and dance hall managements to prevent any repetition of the gang fight started at the weekend by 'Teddy Boys' from London in which three innocent bystanders received nasty injuries. The three victims, all local men, were slashed it is believed with shoe-makers knives, sharpened to a razor edge. Every person seeking admission to the Regent dance hall to-night will be scrutinised by the ballroom manager, Mr Lionel Stewart. "I don't have to bar everybody that looks like a Teddy Boy, but I shall sort them out and those with big rings on just won't get in".¹⁰

As the decade progressed, this association with violence was cemented into the nation's consciousness when the films *Blackboard Jungle* and *Rock Around the Clock* were shown in Britain in 1955 and 1956. Cinema seats were ripped out and young people flouted convention and danced in the aisles of cinemas up and down the land.

In *Folk Devils and Moral Panics* Stanley Cohen describes how 'teenage delinquency' in post-war Britain became the moral panic of the day and Teddy Boys, the disaffected youth of the 1950s, were crowned the folk devils. However much sociologists, and indeed Cohen himself, may have distanced themselves from aspects of this book, much of this seminal text still has resonance. The media, eager to sensationalise the smallest and most insignificant of events, perpetuated a myth, a panic over teenage delinquency with lurid tales of promiscuity, criminality and above all violence. Cohen explains that whilst it was clear that the government and media thought there was a problem with teenagers, less obvious was the cause, or the remedy:

> Each society possesses a set of ideas about what causes deviation – is it due, say, to sickness or to wilful perversity? – and a set of images of who constitutes the typical deviant – is he an innocent lad being led astray, or is he a psychopathic thug? – and these conceptions shape what is done about the behaviour.[11]

Nature or nurture, what has caused the Teddy Boy phenomena? Written off by society because of this Ted-equals-violence equation, Cohen argues that this became a self-fulfilling prophecy. MP Sir Alexander Spearman, speaking at Conservative party conference in Scarborough in 1958, blamed a crime wave 'on these so-called Teddy Boys, because they never had the stick'. He advocated that 'on conviction they should be fined tremendously heavily and, if unable to pay, be made to work and work and work until they can pay off the fine'.[12]

Possessing an incredible twenty-twenty foresight, Sir William Robson-Brown, Conservative MP for Esher, Surrey, predicted that 'the Teddy Boy of today is likely to be the irresponsible shop-steward of tomorrow'.[13] Nationally, the Conservative party proposed Teddy Boy jails designed to 'de-Teddy the Teddy Boys as a way to solve the problems of British youth,'[14] to take the stuffing out of the Teddies, so to speak. However ridiculous this may seem today, this was the moral panic of the time. The problem of teenage delinquency was currency and was heavily reported in the local and national press. Cohen again:

The media have long operated as agents of moral indignation in their own right: even if they are not self-consciously engaged in crusading or muck-raking, their very reporting of certain 'facts' can be sufficient to generate concern, anxiety, indignation or panic.[15]

When it came to the reportage of the Notting Hill riots and the involvement of Teddy Boys, the media travelled down what would become a familiar path: 'The real causes of [the riot] appear to be principally in the boredom and frustration experienced by our Teddy boys... Coloured people are simply a convenient and often defenceless target for aggression'.[16]

If for just one moment, we substitute the words Teddy Boys and coloured people for Mods and Clacton an uncanny similarity unfolds. A bank holiday weekend, a group of teenagers who are bored and a lack of facilities. This could be exactly what Cohen was referring to when he reflected years later in his description of the first mods versus rockers confrontations in Clacton on Easter bank holiday in 1964. Cohen then goes on to describe the use of emotive language for dramatic effect in the reporting of the Whitson bank holiday 'riots' in Hastings later that summer, what he called 'over-reporting':

> The regular use of phrases such as 'riot', 'orgy of destruction', 'battle', 'attack', 'siege', 'beat up the town' and 'screaming mob' left an image of a besieged town from which innocent holidaymakers were fleeing to escape a marauding mob.[17]

Again, change the word holidaymakers for coloureds [sic] and we see a pattern emerging on how disturbances are presented by the media. Nuanced and evocative reporting sets the stage, all that changes are the actors. From a sociological perspective there are similarities between the perceptions of both Teddy Boys and the 'coloured' community in what Cohen calls volatility. 'Successful moral panics owe their appeal to their ability to find points of resonance with wider anxieties.'[18] The inference is that Teddy Boys were symptomatic of a wider malaise in society: 'it's not only this but...it's been building up over the years...it will get worse if nothing's done'. Precisely the same language used by the media when discussing Caribbean immigration.

Whatever similarities there may be between the overall media commentary at the time of the three events described – the Notting Hill riots, and the mod versus rocker skirmishes in Clacton and Hastings – and whether or not boredom might have played its part in the bank holiday events, this should not diminish the real and violent racist attacks that occurred in August 1958. Nor should it cloud the response from the government. Desperate to assuage any accusation of 'racialism' endemic in British society or accept that the appalling conditions people were living in had a part to play, the government and the national media needed to find another reason for the disturbances in 1958. Fortunately, 'deviance' in the guise of the Teddy Boy was at hand. However inaccurate and overblown some of the reports were, the fact remains that Teddy Boys were active in and around the riots of 1958. Television, newspaper and police reports all carry stories and photographs of gangs of Teds armed and looking for trouble. Files from the Metropolitan police during the summer of 1958 show disproportionately higher arrests of the Ted to the non-Ted variety. Their involvement takes George Melly's statement 'what starts as revolt finishes as style' and turned it on its head; in this instance fashion had morphed into rebellion.

Notes

1   For reasons of space, I am unable to go into any detail re the Nottingham riots, although they impacted upon British society as well. The same underlying causes were behind the riots in both Nottingham and Notting Hill. However, as SCIF operated mainly in London it is here that I will focus.

2   The *Kensington Post* 8 August 1958. The men were arrested just round the corner in The Goldhawk Club in Shepherds Bush which went on to become the home for The Who only 6 years later.

3   We will look at police reports later.

4   The *Kensington News* 19 September 1959.

5   Foot (1965) p132.

6   Ibid p162.

7   Cohen (2009) p28.

8   *http://edwardianteddyboy.com*

9   Longhurst (2009) p97.

10   *Brighton Herald* 20 November 1954.

11   Cohen (2009) p7.

12   *The Daily Worker* 23 October 1958.

13   *The Daily Worker* 9 January 1959.

14   Ibid.

15   Cohen (2009) p7.

16   *The Times* 5 September 1958.

17   Cohen (2009) p20.

18   Ibid p7.

05: Great Balls of Fire

WHATEVER THE difficulties Teddy Boys were having as teenagers, and whatever problems were being faced by West Indians integrating into their new society, these issues were soon exploited and exacerbated by organised fascists who began operating in Notting Hill toward the mid-1950s. Although never disappearing completely, the various grouplets of far right activists had been dormant in the wider political arena since their defeat by the 43 Group at the end of the 1940s. Whilst Mosley had spent much of his time in prison learning German, he tactically distanced himself from Hitler and using the term 'fascism' at the war's end. He sensed that the industrial, genocidal slaughter of millions of people solely on the basis of their faith, did not make for good public relations. At the beginning of the new decade his anti-Semitism was not having the resonance it once had. Alongside Mosley, other familiar faces reappeared and began organising in west London, but this time, around the issues of immigration and the crumbling of empire.

Arnold Leese based his post-war operations in Notting Hill. Leese was mentor to a younger equally fanatical Nazi named Colin Jordan, who had earned his stripes as Leese's foot soldier in the 1940s. Splitting from the League of Empire Loyalists (LEL), a far right pressure group formed in 1954 to 'defend the empire', Jordan created the White Defence League (WDL) in September 1958. The WDL were 'rabid in their racial hatred' and swiftly began a sustained agitation and propaganda campaign, 'Keep Britain White'.[1]

Leese died in 1956 and left his house to Colin Jordan. Number 74 Princedale Road, W11 – often referred to as Arnold Leese House –

could not have been more ideally situated as a centre of operations for the WDL; it was right in the middle of Notting Hill. From there they distributed their newspaper *Black and White News*. Posters, leaflets and graffiti carrying the message Keep Britain White began appearing all over W11 and their headquarters brazenly displayed their name and logo. Colin Jordan explained their philosophy:

> The objects of the White Defence League are to keep Britain the white man's country that it has always been, to preserve the white civilisation which is the product of our race and to preserve our northern European blood which in our opinion is our greatest national treasure... We believe in the bold and vital step of stopping all coloured immigration into Britain and repatriating with all humane consideration the coloured immigrants who are already here.[2]

The tactics of British fascists in the 1930s and 1940s had been to recruit from the aristocracy via Oxbridge and Whitehall for funds and political influence, the middle class using book reading groups to develop speakers and leadership and the working class to use for its street fighting paramilitary forces. Throughout those twenty years there had been vicious and systematic attacks against Jews from the BUF and the UM. Young working class men were recruited to form terror gangs to intimidate and beat up Jews, trade unionists and left wingers. Incidents of violence were commonplace and no-go areas and unofficial curfews for Jews existed in parts of London. Organised gangs of these street fighters, or Biff Boys as they were known in the 1930s, were replaced by Mosley's and Jordan's Teddy Boys of the 1950s. UM meetings – addressed by radicalised graduates – proliferated, and as the summer of 1958 progressed, violent incidents against black people began being reported to the police. The savagery of some of these attacks has been lost in time. Beatings, razor attacks, stabbings, the windows of black families smashed on a constant basis with the tenants left cowering in fear. A black man attacked in a pub in North Kensington and battered with metal dustbin lids and broken bottles. Another was shot in the leg. Petrol bombs were thrown through windows of houses with pregnant women inside. Gangs of white teenagers roamed the streets of west London with knives, iron bars, sticks and razors, slashing and attacking black people at will. A particularly ugly development was the regular late Saturday night attempts by white drivers to run down black people in their cars, described by the white locals as a 'sport'.[3]

What has now been accepted as the spark for the riots began on the night of Saturday 30 August 1958. After a fracas with her black husband the previous night Majbritt Morrison, a young white Swedish woman, was confronted by a group of white locals unhappy with her marriage to a Jamaican who was allegedly also her pimp. They threw stones and bottles at her and attacked her with an iron bar. Soon afterwards a 400-strong crowd of white men gathered – many of them Teddy Boys – and began attacking houses occupied by West Indians, including a blues party with a sound system run by Count Suckle.[4] Sensing an opportunity, the following day the UM organised an impromptu open air meeting amid the aftermath of the attacks. A reporter from the *Kensington Post* was there:

> In the middle of a mob of screaming, jeering youths and adults, a speaker from the Union Movement was urging his excited audience to "get rid of them" (the coloured people). Groups of policemen stood at strategic points carefully watching the meeting...suddenly hundreds of leaflets were thrown over the crowd. A fierce cry went in the air and the mob rushed off in the direction of Latimer Road shouting "Kill the niggers".[5]

Police eyewitness reports were withheld in secret documents and not released until 2002 when they were obtained by *The Guardian*. They paint a frightening picture:

> The disturbances were overwhelmingly triggered by 300-to 400-strong "Keep Britain White" mobs, many of them Teddy boys armed with iron bars, butcher's knives and weighted leather belts, who went "nigger-hunting" among the West Indian residents of Notting Hill and Notting Dale. The first night left five black men lying unconscious on the pavements of Notting Hill.[6]

Another censured police witness, PC Richard Bedford, provided graphic evidence of the motives of the gangs of youth – some several

September 1958 Teddy Boys and Girls run through Blenheim Crescent, Notting Hill, during the riots in West London.

thousand strong at times – who roamed the streets of Notting Hill, breaking into homes and attacking any West Indian they could find. He said he had seen a mob of 300 to 400 white people in Bramley Road shouting: 'We will kill all black bastards. Why don't you send them home?' PC Ian McQueen on the same night said he was told: 'Mind your own business, coppers. Keep out of it. We will settle these niggers our way. We'll murder the bastards.'[7] The files also revealed that senior police officers at the time had assured the Home Secretary Rab Butler that there was little or no racial motivation behind the disturbances, despite testimony from individual police officers to the contrary.

The 3 September edition of *The Times* reported:

> A big crowd of youths chanting "Down with the niggers" assembled in Lancaster Road and a youth leading one group held up a banner with the slogan "Deport all niggers".[8]

This group of young men, the report continued, had been selling *Action*, the Union Movement's newspaper, and prior to that they had attended a highly charged meeting addressed by Oswald Mosley. The whole of W11 was a war zone. Tony Benn later recalled in his diaries: '...[seeing] the debris and the corrugated iron up behind the windows of the prefabs where the coloured families lived... there is a large area where it is not safe for people to be out'.[9]

What was the official response to the violence? Eager to present itself to the commonwealth as 'enlightened conservatives' the Tory government was not moved to an immediate knee jerk reaction and Rab Butler stated: 'No change would be forced on the government's immigration policies by extremists'[10] However, Tory backbencher Cyril Osborne spoke for many in his party, declaring in the Commons, 'It is time someone spoke for this country and for the white man who lives here and the idleness, sickness and crime that coloured people brought to the country'.[11]

Tony Benn urged Labour leader Hugh Gaitskill to make an intervention, but none was forthcoming. Initially the silence from the Labour Party leadership was deafening.[12] Not so quiet was Notting Hill Labour MP George Rogers, who firmly laid the blame for the riots on the black population and called for tighter immigration controls, a call echoed by then TUC general secretary Vincent Tewson. Rogers went even further in his attacks, blaming West Indians for provoking the 'response' of locals by failing to adapt to the British way of life. He demanded an end to unrestricted immigration, the deportation of anti-social elements and the re-housing of immigrants to stop ghettoes forming. Leading British fascist Jeffery Hamm joked: 'I welcome Mr Rogers' conversion, and look forward to his application for membership'.[13] Later that first week of September, at the friends meeting house in Euston, a huge meeting was addressed by Jamaican first minister Norman Manley, urging black people to stand up for their rights. Also speaking from the top table (or trying to) was George Rogers. His contribution proved somewhat difficult though, as every time 'the Labour MP attempted to speak he was booed, hissed and heckled'.[14]

Rogers was pandering to the outpouring of racism in the aftermath of the riots. A nationwide poll conducted a few days after Notting Hill found that 55% wanted restrictions on immigration; 71% disapproved of 'marriages between white and coloured people'; 54%

wanted people born in Britain to have preference on housing lists; and 61% said they would move house 'if coloured people came to live in great numbers' in their district. This was despite the fact that only 49% of those polled had ever known a non-white person.[15]

The West Indian community had seen the writing on the wall and had begun organising against this level of racism and the violence during the riots. On the bank holiday Monday, a well-known meeting place called Totobags Cafe at 9 Blenheim Crescent became the headquarters of Caribbean defence. A large group of men, including many Jamaicans who had travelled over from Brixton to give solidarity, assembled inside, awaiting the inevitable attack. Baron Baker, in the building at the time and one of the first to be arrested, remembered:

> During the day we made our preparations for the attack and I can quite clearly remember I was standing on the second floor, with the lights out in Blenheim Crescent, when I saw, look out and see from Kensington Park Road to Portobello Road, a massive lot of people out there and I distinctly remember what they say, 'let's burn the niggers, lets lynch the niggers' and from those spoken words, I said 'start bomb them' then we see the Molotov cocktails coming out from number nine Blenheim Crescent.[16]

The disturbances continued night after night until they finally began to peter out on September 5th. In total 108 people were arrested. Later in the year at the Old Bailey, Judge Salmon handed down exemplary sentences of four years and a £500 fine for each of the nine white youths who openly admitted they had gone 'nigger hunting'. Asked by the judge why they had been involved in the violence, this explanation for their actions was offered by one: 'I hate niggers'.[17] The National Labour Party, another small Nazi rump organised a petition opposing the 'severity' of the sentences, collecting 10,000 local signatures in just one week.[18] Sitting alongside the defence in court was Oswald Mosley, who provided funds for the Teds on trial. Ever the opportunist, Mosley was trying to subvert this sub-culture of white working class youth to become a tool to be used by the UM. He would try to exploit their disaffection and champion their cause whilst cynically attempting to use their violent potential for political gain. 'They're fine fellows some of these so-called Teds up in Notting Hill' Mosley said whilst trying to get their sentences remitted on the grounds of their 'good previous character'.[19] Both Mosley and Jordan increased their activity in W11 after the riots. Whilst all around west London groups and organisations were forming, trying to find ways of avoiding further violence and an escalation of antipathy, Mosley and Jordan sought to exacerbate the tensions in the area. As he had done in the 1930s and the 1940s, Mosley was building for another grand event: 1959 was to be an election year and he was to stand in North Kensington.

Notes

1   Thurlow (1987) p263.

2   *Panorama* 13 April 1959.

3   Glass (1960) p134.

4   Count Suckle was a Jamaica-born sound system operator and club owner who was influential in the development of ska and reggae music, and African-Caribbean culture, in the United Kingdom.

5   The *Kensington Post* 4 September 1958.

6   http://www.theguardian.com/uk/2002/aug/24/artsandhumanities. nottinghillcarnival2002

7   Ibid.

8   Glass (1960) p140.

9   p.1 https://books.google.co.uk/books

10   Ibid.

11   *Daily Mail*, 8 June 2013.

12   The Labour Party did later issue a statement unambiguously rejecting immigration controls and promising the next Labour government would 'introduce legislation making illegal the public practice of discrimination'.

13   https://books.google.co.uk/books. p1

14   Ibid.

15   *Daily Mail*, 8 June 2013.

16   https://www.youtube.com/watch?v=LvhkOokRm-I

17   Vague (2003) p89.

18   John Bean formed The National Labour Party, yet another Nazi party in 1957, merged it with the WDL in 1960 and he eventually ended up in the National Front, finally becoming a leading member of The British National Party.

19   The *Kensington News* and *West London Times*, 26 September 1958.

06: Smoke Gets in Your Eyes

THE MUSICIANS UNION (MU) had been groundbreaking in its response to racism. In 1947 it passed a resolution at its annual conference declaring that it would oppose the colour bar wherever it appeared. The union was one of the first organisations to demand a boycott of apartheid in South Africa. MU initiatives were integral to opposing racism in dance halls and after a sustained campaign the colour bar was lifted in Mecca ballrooms in Nottingham, Birmingham, Streatham and Sheffield on 16 October 1958. After the August bank holiday violence, the reaction from musicians was swift. Aside from the predictable statements issued by the established political parties in the national and local media, the first real responses to the riots came from musicians. There were two weekly musical newspapers in Britain at the time, the *New Musical Express*, which was orientated toward the teenage pop and rock n roll market and the *Melody Maker*, a more earnest publication that concentrated on folk, blues and jazz. The following appeal appeared on the front page of *Melody Maker* on 5 September 1958, just a day after the trouble had finally subsided:

> At a time when reason has given way to violence in parts of Britain, we, the people of all races in the world of entertainment, appeal to the public to reject racial discrimination in any shape or form. Violence will settle nothing: it will only cause suffering to innocent people and create fresh grievances. We appeal to our audiences everywhere to join us in opposing any and every aspect of colour prejudice wherever it may appear.[1]

In the same edition, music critic and independent record producer

Denis Preston demanded that 'something is needed, roughly on the lines of America's National Association for the Advancement of Colored People to articulate the concerns of the black population'.[2] Agreeing with Preston was folk singer Fred Dallas who:

Wants to form a committee of big name entertainers and get out a statement protesting against mob violence and prejudice, then the permanent organisation can follow. Already a body exists called the British-Caribbean Welfare Service. Maybe it can assist in the birth of Britain's NAACP. I am confident the Musicians Union and a great many jazz players and listeners would support such a movement.[3]

By the following week *Melody Maker* declared:

Letters, telephone messages, even telegrams and personal callers offering support have come into this office from all directions since last Friday. They confirm that in the jazz world there is a lot of racial tolerance and at present, indignation about the whipped-up outbursts of anti-colour feeling waiting to be tapped.[4]

A two-page article written by Frank Sinatra also appeared in that week's edition of *Melody Maker* under the title: 'Frank Sinatra says Jazz Has No Colour Bar'. Fred Dallas had now teamed up with Johnny Dankworth and Cleo Laine and with the addition of industry friends Winifred Atwell, Ken Colyer, Max Jones, George Melly, Russell Quaye and Hylda Sims they formed the Stars Campaign for Interracial Friendship (SCIF). At its initial meeting early that September, the decision was made to appoint a chair, they opted for the most high profile member they knew and Laurence Olivier took the job, with Johnny Dankworth as vice-chair.[5] The organisation was loose but they decided its strategy would be to organise around the single issue of racism and use the celebrity of its members to promote racial harmony. Author Eric Hobsbawm was later to say: 'The purpose of SCIF… was to articulate through the combined presence of music and culture, and left activists and writers, a cultural policy of racial inclusion and social solidarity at a time of crisis'.[6]

They also agreed that a statement in opposition to the racism behind the riots was needed. An appeal in an eight-page illustrated broadsheet *What The Stars Say* was produced and handed around jazz clubs in the West End and the Notting Hill area. It was SCIF's mission statement, the campaign intended to promote:

> The ideals of racial tolerance and harmony through the example of those who earn their living in the world of art and entertainment, and in the associated realms of journalism, writing and the productive side of show business. Its aims are: to promote understanding between races and banish ignorance about racial characteristics; to combat instances of social prejudice by verbal and written protests; to set an example to the general public through members personal race relations; and to use all available means to publicise their abhorrence of racial discrimination.[7]

Local newspaper the *Kensington Post* carried a headline on 3 October announcing that SCIF was the 'only unofficial body to publicly condemn the riots...[and] had held several meetings at Johnny Dankworth's premises in Denmark Street – the home of Tin Pan Alley'. Hylda Sims remembers:

> There were a few meetings at Johnny Dankworth's office, I think it was in Tin-Pan Alley. It was here that I first met Johnny and Cleo, also Francis Newton, which was Eric Hobsbawm's jazz name. I remember MacInnes, Colin MacInnes being there and after these meetings he would go leafleting around Notting Hill. From here we organised activities and some gigs.[8]

The *Post* reported that SCIF intended to hold these concerts in London with guest appearances from national celebrities. The first gig at Soho's Skiffle Cellar is recalled by SCIF founder Fred Dallas:

> It was a fundraiser in Soho, on a weekday night where we assembled and were blown away by this very tall white kid who sounded like an old delta bluesman, but he had the most amazing voice... it was Long John Baldry.[9]

Hylda Sims again:

> We did a fundraiser, somewhere around Leicester Square in a big club with a stage, [most likely this was Ken Colyer's Studio

51 in Great Newport Street] it was mine and Russell [Quaye's] group The City Ramblers, we also did another couple of gigs around Soho.[10]

The first high profile SCIF event was a Christmas party for children of all races picked from three local schools on 23 December 1958 in Holland Park School, W8. Over two hundred and fifty children attended from the West Indian, Irish, African and English communities. Music was provided by SCIF members. The event was also attended by the Mayor and London County Council vice-chair. The local press covered the festivities and according to the *Kensington News*, the day was a great success. The food and drink was provided by the American Embassy – who really, in 1958, were in no position to be talking about integrated lunches – and the BBC televised the party, the recording of which, sadly, is now lost.

SCIF's first permanent initiative was to found a club to promote interracial mixing and openly oppose the colour bar. The Harmony Club opened its doors on 19 January 1959. Josephine Douglas, SCIF member, actress and co-host of Britain's first pop chart television show *Six-Five Special*, hosted the club alongside actor Harvey Hall. SCIF's simple yet ambitious aim for the club was articulated by Jo Douglas: 'to bring racial harmony to the Notting Hill Gate area'.[11] Also present on the opening night were jazz singer Rosemary Squires and Caribbean folklorist and singer Edric Connor. Rosemary Squires recalls the evening:

> I was asked by one of the presenters of the show Six-Five Special, a popular lady called Jo Douglas, to visit a young people's youth club, a multi-racial club, I suppose as a morale booster, which I gladly did. This is where the photo of me was taken and the other person was another singer of the day, a very nice gentleman, named Edric Connor.[12]

A special message of support was sent from Paul Robeson and was read out at the opening.[13] The *Kensington Post* reported on the night:

> White and coloured children hammered on the door of St Marks Church Hall Notting Hill, on Monday evening. But they had to stay outside to listen to the beat of the bongo drums and

the rhythm of the top-class jazz for it was invitation only at the opening session of the Harmony Club. Inside the hall was packed tight with singing, stamping and jiving teenagers of all races.

There was only one colour problem at the club – started by the Stars Campaign for Interracial Friendship – and that was the possibility of getting wet paint on clothes. Right up to the last moment the youngsters in the working party had been busy cleaning up the church hall and putting on new bright paint. Over the weekend television personality Josephine Douglas helped with the work. Very soon 'Joe' was an old friend of the boys and girls. This helped to make the show a very formal affair.

The juke-box is already part of the club's equipment, but there was no need to put on records. Music was provided on stage by Jonnie Dankworth, Rosemary Squires and coloured singers Edric Connor, Frank Holder and 'Cuddly' Dudley Heslop. Before the youngsters pushed back the chairs for jiving, TV actor Harvey Hall, the chairman spoke about the club. He said: 'you can use a lot of high-sounding words. But all it comes down to is getting to know each other better.[14]

The club promised to open twice a week on Mondays and Fridays and Johnny Dankworth, Cleo Laine, Humphrey Lyttelton and Dickie Valentine, amongst others, would attend and perform. Not only was this club open to all – irrespective of race – it positively encouraged 'young people of all races together in a non-political, non-sectarian social club'.[15] Black and white people would meet each other, talk to each other and most importantly dance with each other. Furthermore, chairman Harvey Hall told the *Post*:

There will be weekly meetings and the youngsters will have a say in the running of the club. And they will be asked to bring their friends in. But this will not be a select club, we do want to bring the rougher element in, Teddy boys will be welcomed.[16]

Jo Douglas: 'This club isn't a deep thing. It's essentially a social club. We want young people of different races, nationalities and creeds to get together and enjoy themselves'.[17] Looking into the future Hall hoped that this club 'may lead to a chain of Harmony Clubs

Above: Chris Barber, centre, on trombone and Lonnie Donegan, second left on banjo
Below: Ronnie Scott, left, and Tubby Hayes

bringing white and coloured people together all over London and in other parts of the country'.[18] The Harmony Club was not alone in its endeavors to ease racial tensions, as community clubs and integration groups began appearing in the area, but because of the celebrity status of SCIF's members and the sheer amount of stars it recruited, it was guaranteed to draw the biggest headlines. This was calculated, it was part of the SCIF strategy from the start.[19]

It is difficult to comprehend the climate at this time, and understand how provocative the setting up of an interracial club must have been to some white people, notwithstanding the fascist presence in the area. The calls for repatriation rang from every corner in the streets around the Harmony Club. It was a brave decision both physically and politically to make Blenheim Crescent the club's home as the street had been at the centre of the racial violence only months before. According to Trevor Grundy's *Memoir of a Fascist Childhood*: 'Several hundred Teds [had] joined the Notting Hill branch of the [Union] movement.'[20] So the very people responsible for the racist violence were sought by SCIF to frequent their racially inclusive club. It would of course have been pointless setting up an interracial club where there was no racial diversity, superfluous to ease tension where none existed, so Notting Hill was the only logical place the club could locate. This does not, however, negate the courage of those who made it happen.[21]

The importance of London as a place is also relevant here, as music historian Sara Cohen explains:

> The dynamic interrelationship between music and place... suggests that music plays a very particular and sensual role in the production of place partly through its peculiar embodiment of movement and collectivity.[22]

Why did SCIF occur in London, why didn't it happen in Nottingham? There had been riots there; and there was also Caribbean migration, Nottingham also had a small jazz and skiffle scene. Of course London geographically is a much bigger city, but in terms of creating the dynamic that Cohen talks about, bigger does not necessarily mean better as it can create problems in travel, cost, communication and even finding out that there are others who share your interests. This I believe explains why Soho became so important for the music scene and SCIF in London. A gravitational pull to the centre of the city, where everyone from the outskirts can meet and all clubs are within walking distance. Soho did not create a 'scene' and a 'scene' did not create Soho, but the two were utterly interdependent. Peterson and Bennett's explanation of what a scene is:

A focused social activity that takes place in a delimited space and over a specific span of time in which clusters of producers, musicians, and fans realise their common musical taste, collectively distinguishing themselves by using music and other cultural signs often appropriated from other places, but recombined and developed in ways that come to represent the local scene. The focused activity we are interested in here, of course, centres on a particular style of music, but such music scenes characteristically involve other diverse lifestyle elements as well. These usually include a distinctive style of dancing, a particular range of psychoactive drugs, style of dress, politics and the like.[23]

The Soho jazz scene fulfils each of these criteria, and the detachment of the jazz scene from wider 'square' society may have had political implications and an input into the identification the musicians had with other 'outside' groups like West Indian immigrants. Place becomes important also when we look at the specificity of the riots. They did not and could not have happened in Soho, as the area is too small to accommodate any sizeable migration, but it did have a scene. Notting Hill could cope with immigration, but it did not have a jazz scene where musicians could congregate. That Soho was the home of London jazz may also partly explain later criticisms of the activities of SCIF as being gesture politics, what is now colloquially called 'parachuting in' activists not native to an area. Whilst a valid criticism, this cannot be levelled at all SCIF members, notably Colin MacInnes, who lived and worked tirelessly in and around Notting Hill throughout the period. According to Hobsbawm: 'MacInnes went about the area, a favourite stamping ground of his, posting its news-sheet through letter boxes.'[24] In Golds biography of the author, Victor Musgrove:

poet, art dealer and friend recalls MacInnes driving round Notting Hill posting *What The Stars Say* through letterboxes and being convinced that this had prevented further rioting.

Notes
1   This statement was initially signed by 27 celebrities: Larry Adler, Chris Barber, Pearl Carr, Alma Cogan, Johnny Dankworth, Lonnie Donegan, Charlie Drake, Ray Ellington, Tubby Hayes, Ted Heath (band leader), Teddy Johnson, Cleo Laine, Humphrey Lyttelton, Matt Monroe, Mick Mulligan, Otilie Patterson, Marion Ryan, Ronnie Scott, Harry Seacombe, Peter Sellers, Tommy Steele, Eric Sykes, Dickie Valentine, Frankie Vaughan, Kent Walton, David Whitfield, Marty Wilde. It also became an appeal that was distributed in jazz clubs and the Notting Hill area.

2   *Melody Maker* 6 September 1958. Founding SCIF member Karl Dallas told this writer that without Preston SCIF would never have happened. Telephone interview 06/07/15.

3   Ibid.

4   *Melody Maker* 13 September 1958.

5   Karl Dallas told this writer, Olivier was happy to be a signatory on condition he played absolutely no part in SCIF's activities. Telephone interview Karl Dallas: 06/07/2015.

6   *http://www.camdennewjournal.com/feature-books-how-change-world-tales-marx-and-marxism-eric-hobsbawm*. There were also Sports Personalities who signed a similar statement of support in response to the riots. (They were – Danny Blanchflower, Jimmy Hill, Jack Crump, Joe Erskine, Thelma Hopkins, Derek Ibbotson, George Knight, Stanley Matthews, Ken Norris, Frank Sando, David Sheppard, and Alan Wharton).

7   Glass (1960) p198.

8   Telephone Interview Hylda Sims: 02/09/2015.

9   Telephone interview Karl Dallas: 06/07/2015.

10   Telephone Interview Hylda Sims: 02/09/2015.

11   *Melody Maker* 20 December 1958.

12   Email interview Rosemary Squires 19/08/2015.

13   I was unable to find a copy of this message.

14   *Kensington Post* 23 January 1959.

15   *Kensington Post* 16 January 1959.

16   Ibid.

17   Ibid.

18   Ibid.

19   For a full list of SCIF members see appendix ii.

20   Grundy (1999) p199.

21   Both black and white activists received death threat letters from fascist groups on a regular basis and several arson threats were made to burn the hall that housed the club to the ground. Sherwood. (1999) p116.

22   Sarah Cohen, 'Sounding out the City: Music and the sensuous production of place', *Transactions of the Institute of British Geographers*, Vol 20, No 4 (1995) p434.

23   Longhurst (2007) p252

24   *http://www.rulit.me/books/interesting-times-a-twentieth-century-life-read-233799-68.html*

07: What a Difference a Day Makes

SCIF WAS NOT the only
organisation operating in the Notting Hill area. There were other
initiatives organised by a variety of groups, the largest being the
Coloured Peoples Progressive Association (CPPA) founded by
activist Frances Ezzrecco. Alongside this was the Association for the
Advancement of Coloured People (AACP) formed by Amy Ashwood
Garvey, co-founder of the American Universal Negro Improvement
Association, one-time director of the Black Star Line and first wife
of Marcus Garvey. The People's National Movement (PNM), the
Africa League (AL), the African-Asian Congress (AAC), St Peters
Coloured People's Group (SCPG), The *West Indian Gazette* (WIG)
and the Indian Workers Association (IWA) all had parts to play. The
local council employed a West Indian welfare worker 'as a first step
to reducing inter-racial tension'. The Mayor promised a 'Goodwill
Week' sometime in the summer of 1959 where a variety of music,
food, costume and culture would be celebrated.[1] A demonstration
for interracial fellowship was also organised in Trafalgar Square by
the Movement for Colonial Freedom. SCIF was either active in, or
actually on, many of the events organised by the above groups.

Here we have to take some time to understand why SCIF or
at least some of its members were able to be immersed in local
Caribbean organisations in Notting Hill. This can be explained
by the input of one woman, Claudia Jones. Born a Trinidadian in
1915, her family moved to New York when she was nine years old.
At aged twenty-one she joined the Young Communist League of
America, twelve years later she was on the National Executive of

the American Communist Party (CPUSA). Politically active at the height of the McCarthyite witch-hunts, after several sojourns to the state penitentiary she was deported from the US in 1955 and chose England as her new home. A seasoned political campaigner Claudia took no time in becoming active in her adopted London. Gravitating toward the Communist Party (CP), here she met Eric Hobsbawm, CP member, academic, historian and SCIF member. Years later Hobsbawm had this to say about Jones:

> While it lasted, it [SCIF] enjoyed the invaluable help of the remarkably able and admirable Claudia Jones, a US Communist Party functionary born in the West Indies and expelled as a 'non-citizen' from the US in the witch-hunt days, who did her best, with indifferent success, to bring some Party efficiency and some political structure into the Caribbean immigration in West London and to get adequate backing for her efforts from the British CP. An impressive woman.[2]

Her relationship with the Communist Party, however, was to prove fraught. The CP issued the '*Charter of Rights for Coloured Workers of Britain* in 1955. There were four main points to the charter:

— Racial discrimination should be a penal offence

— Government restrictions and discrimination against coloured workers should be opposed

— There must be equality in employment, wages and conditions

— Coloured workers should join appropriate trade unions on equal terms to white workers.

The CP produced 150,000 leaflets and pamphlets to this effect. They proclaimed 'No Colour Bar for Britain'. Also by 1956 a West Indies Committee of the Communist Party had been set up. However, anti-racist work did not always appear to be prioritised by the rest of the party and even leading CP members like Eric Hobsbawm seem to have been involved in anti-racist work almost by accident, via music rather than political principle:

> With the American civil rights movements and the influx of coloured immigrants to Britain, racism became a far more central

theme on the left than it had been. Through jazz I found myself associated with an early anti-racist campaign [SCIF] in Britain after the so-called Notting Hill race riots of 1958.[3]

The Communist Party's charter of rights struggled to find practical application. In the Kentish Town (North London) by-election in the winter of 1958, the Conservative, Labour and Communist candidates agreed to keep race out of the forthcoming election. Unfortunately, a fourth candidate, publican William Webster, didn't and stood as an independent on a 'Keep Kentish Town White' platform.[4]

For Claudia Jones the attitude of the CP, however well intentioned, fell short of the task at hand. Indeed, fellow West Indian CP member Billy Strachan commented: 'the party itself did not know what racism was.'[5] The analysis of the CP toward West Indians residing in Britain in the 1950s was framed by two things: one, the so-called colonial struggles – the national movements of indigenous peoples in the Americas, Africa and Asia against British Imperial rule – and two, an economic determinism that saw class division as the singular division in society. The latter did not identify the particular oppression suffered by black and Asian people inside and outside of the UK, how that oppression distorts their class position and how discrimination works as an ancillary to the class system that the CP had identified. In their weekly publication *World News* the CP commented that, as black and Asian workers had only come to the UK to escape the poverty caused by imperialism:

The real solution to the problem [of race relations] is to free the colonies and end imperialist exploitation, so that the colonial workers can freely build up their own countries and reap the benefits of the wealth which they produce.[6]

Evan Smith points out in his *Science & Society* article:

This statement lends to the notion, pervasive in the 1950s, that black immigrants were the "problem." By favouring struggles in the colonies, the CPGB avoided making any serious suggestions for tackling the problems faced by those immigrants in Britain, and in doing so confounded the issues of racial discrimination and the effects of imperialism.[7]

Consequently, much of Claudia Jones' emphasis was to work inside the various black groups in London that existed at the time and to concentrate on two in particular, the AACP and the CPPA. Afro-Caribbean groups both, they were engaged in political work at a local and national level especially around attempts to enact legislation in parliament which would outlaw racial discrimination. Jones campaigned tirelessly against racism, in housing; education and employment, addressed demonstrations, peace rallies and the Trade Union Congress.

However, she shall always be remembered for two massive contributions to anti-racism and black political history in the UK. In April 1958 Jones set up the *West Indian Gazette and Afro-Asian Caribbean News* (WIG). This was the first wholly black newspaper in Britain. She saw the paper as:

> A catalyst, quickening the awareness, socially and politically, of West Indians, Afro-Asians and their friends. Its editorial stand is for a united, independent West Indies, full economic, social and political equality and respect for human dignity for West Indians and Afro-Asians in Britain, and for peace and friendship between all Commonwealth and world peoples.[8]

Arguing a consistent political line against racism, the newspaper was an important political forum, but it also served a cultural need – it was a focus for displaced people feeling homesick and seeking solace, inside their own community, from a hostile environment. Towering over all her other achievements was the creation of the Notting Hill Carnival. Organised specifically to make a cultural and political statement that black people were here to stay in Britain. Carnival was Jones and her associates' attempt to use this Caribbean tradition as a tool of political defiance and cultural seduction. As an early member of SCIF Claudia Jones had already seen this combination utilised with the Harmony Club and gigs and events in Soho. Carnival in Britain, like the prototype from Trinidad, was to be a celebration of Afro-Caribbean, food, dress, music and dance. Understanding the delicate nature of the political situation vis-a-vis white and black residents of Nottingham and Notting Hill just months after the riots, the front page of the Carnival brochure fan-fared the event but also carried an important political message: 'part of the proceeds [from the sale] of this brochure are to assist the payments of fines of coloured and white youths involved in the Notting Hill events'. This was political pragmatism; whatever Jones and the other carnival organisers may have thought about the Teddy Boys' violent rampage and their open racism, Carnival was to be an ointment that eased the pain. Despite the fact that the first Carnival was held in freezing cold January, despite the fact it was held indoors in St Pancras town hall, and despite it being organised inside only twelve weeks, it was a huge success. They repeated this success the following year and carnival has now grown into the largest free event in Europe.

Meanwhile, the Harmony Club – despite its best intentions – lasted only six weeks and ceased activities on 9 March 1959 after an acrimonious split between Jo Douglas and Alexis Korner over the running of the club. Douglas had said on national TV that the club had been a failure due to the 'un-clubable' nature of the dead-end kids who were its members. A furious Alexis Korner was 'indignant' saying 'he wished to entirely disassociate himself from Jo Douglas' comments'. Furthermore, Korner argued, 'The trouble was the club was too successful, we were limited to fifty and got hundreds.' He added that, 'he had already made preliminary moves to open a new club for young people of all races in the area'. Asked if it would be a successor to the Harmony Club Korner replied, 'No – I hope it will be an antidote'.[8] Commenting in 1964 on why even the most sincere of the community and race relation projects failed, journalist Paul Foot suggested:

> The main stumbling block to success in such ventures is the "tea and buns" approach. All too often, a local authority or church group decides to sponsor a multi-racial committee, and provides a hall for the purpose. There is an opening party. Invitations are sent out to all known West Indians or to all the "Singhs" on the electoral roll. The Mayor attends, together with other civic dignitaries, as do a band of West Indian students and a few middle class Indians. There are a couple of speeches, a few cups

of tea, everyone applauds and goes home, and soon afterwards the project collapses.[9]

Also writing concomitantly was sociologist Ruth Glass who observed:

> While the [SCIF] campaign had a rather energetic "newsworthy" start [the Christmas party] since then it has been rather quiet.[10]

Others commentating on SCIF's campaign and similar 'friendship' endeavours accused them of 'gesture politics and short-term solutions'.[11] Reflecting years later Eric Hobsbawm concluded:

> Stars Campaign for Interracial Friendship [was] not so much a real political operation…[it was] an example of the modern media operation which, like others of its kind, fizzled out after a few months of rather successful publicity. It did indeed mobilize the "stars", mainly of jazz – most of the big British names were there, Johnny Dankworth and Cleo Laine, Humphrey Lyttelton and Chris Barber, as well as some pop stars – but its strength lay in the operators who could get stories into the press and programmes on to television, and produced newsworthy ideas such as the televised interracial children's Christmas party of 1958.[12]

Nevertheless, there were still attempts to find a winning club formula. Korner went on to set up a new venue in the Paddington area for an older, paying clientele. The City Ramblers skiffle group played regular SCIF gigs in Leicester Square alongside Cleo Laine. A new weekly SCIF club had been established at The Skiffle Cellar, 49 Greek Street, Soho. Humphrey Lyttelton, jazz trumpeter, music journalist and SCIF member, wrote the following piece entitled 'Integration in Soho' in his column in *Melody Maker* on 28 March 1959:

> The regular SCIF parties held in Russell Quaye's 'The Cellar Club' in Soho are becoming a standard event in the London jazz calendar. SCIF – The Stars Campaign for Interracial Friendship – holds these informal parties as a medium through which people of all races can meet each other in a relaxed social atmosphere. The music is suitable hetrodox, ranging from 'spasm' through Caribbean folk song to modern jam session. Though the first

party in February was a tentative affair, launched on a modest scale without much trumpeting from the rooftops, the old reliable grapevine went into operation and brought a continuous stream of guest musicians on to the bandstand during the evening... As the evening progressed and the rum and coca cola flowed the two groups became inextricably entangled and at the climax of the evening, we all set off round the room in a spontaneous procession, followed by a winding, kaleidoscopic crocodile of dancers. The SCIF parties are rapidly establishing the right atmosphere for a similar outbreak of spontaneous combustion. When it happens Soho and its precincts may witness a "racial disturbance" of an altogether happy and festive nature. Being of a generous and expansive frame of mind, we might even wind our joyful way to Notting Hill and serenade Sir Oswald Mosley in his electoral headquarters.[13]

The Harmony Club and the Skiffle Cellar were examples of how SCIF used music and dancing as a political tool against racism and the far right. However tame these events may now seem by modern standards, for 1959 it was groundbreaking. The colour bar was being openly challenged and music was at the heart of it. These small interracial dances proved that integration could work. But some in Westminster were uneasy with any racial mixing at all and politicians who had been arguing for stricter controls on immigration before the riots, had renewed vigour after them. Behind the scenes there were sinister forces afoot. A secret civil service committee had been convened in the mid-1950s by the Conservative government, the Immigration and Repatriation Commonwealth and Coloured Colonials Home Office Working Party. Conservative MP and Under-Secretary of State K B Paice was its chair. Its brief was to seek evidence that non-white immigrants had undesirable characteristics to help make the case for stricter controls.[14] 'Evidence' collated from this working party would be used to push through the Immigration Act of 1962.

The White Defence League had intensified their demonstrations and meetings around Notting Hill. Keep Britain White leaflets, posters and graffiti were everywhere, to such a degree that the weekly documentary programme produced by the BBC, *Panorama*, ran a feature on them on Monday 13 April 1959. WDL leader Colin Jordan explained:

> Naturally we shall try and smooth the repatriation with every humane consideration. We appreciate of course that there are bound to be inconveniences and discomforts, but against that we have to say, the ultimate future of our nation, and if mass coloured immigration continues as it is doing now it will inevitably lead to a coffee coloured half-breed Britain of the future and we are going to fight to stop that.[15]

The second part of the programme centred on SCIF and had interviews with four of its leading members to counteract Jordan. Band leader, saxophonist and vice-chair of SCIF Johnny Dankworth explained what the organisation was all about:

> Well, the objectives of the campaign are largely to counteract any cranky organisations which try to preach the gospel of a master race anywhere. Such organisations such as Mr whats-a-names [Colin Jordan] seem laughable on the face of it but they aren't really laughable because Adolf Hitler started a similar organisation about 20 or 25 years ago which caused the deaths of millions and millions of people the sufferings of millions more.[16]

Asked why he had become involved in SCIF Lonnie Donegan replied: 'In my little span of life I've come across such a sea of bigotries and prejudices that I get so fed up with now that I have to do something about it'.[17] *Panorama* then interviewed jazz singer Cleo Laine:

> *Panorama:* Now it was put to me earlier by the spokesman for the White Defence League that coloured people ought to be repatriated from this country to their country of origin. Now where were you born for instance?
>
> *Cleo Laine :* Southall, Middlesex, or [affects accent] 'Sarfall' Middlesex
>
> *Panorama:* So in fact you are a Londoner, you're an Englishman? [sic]

Cleo Laine: Yes

Panorama: Where would you be, if you had to be repatriated, where would that be to?

Cleo Laine: Southall, Middlesex [laughs][18]

SCIF member and author of *To Sir With Love* E R Braithwaite was asked if the sort of language used by the WDL discouraged or upset him. He replied:

> Not for a moment, you see it indicates to me the strength of British democracy that Mr Jordan or his associates can say this sort of thing and they are free to say it. It also indicates to me that democracy means something to the British people they can contain this sort of thing, just as a healthy body can contain a boil or a pimple if it becomes painful then they'll take steps to deal with it.[19]

That SCIF had been given such a large part in *Panorama*, the BBC's flagship political magazine programme, is an indication of just what they had achieved in such a short time. Their tactics of using their celebrity to highlight injustice and expose racism and fascism had been very successful. It is worth emphasising here just how important this coverage was and how far reaching SCIF's profile became. BBC1 was the only nationwide broadcaster in the UK in 1959. Its solitary competitor, ITV, had been operational for only four years and was still regional in its output. The UK population was around 51 million in the late 1950s, and of that number it was estimated:

> ...[that] the adult television public numbered about 19.5 million, and that viewers spent on average nearly 40 per cent of each evening watching television. Those who had a choice of programmes spent one-third of the time devoted to television watching BBC programmes.[20]

By any standards these are massive viewing figures and SCIF was appearing in the BBCs most important current affairs programme, guaranteeing it an audience of millions. But the high profile TV work did not stop there. *Six-Five Special* was Britain's first teenage rock n roll program, running for two years from 1957. Broadcast at five minutes past six on a Saturday night, its intention was to capture the new teenage market before they went out dancing or to the cinema. Its audience was eight million people each week. *Six-Five Special's* presenters were Jo Douglas and Pete Murray. Both were in SCIF. The cast of the programme reads like the membership list of SCIF: Jim Dale, Johnny Dankworth, Tubby Hayes, Ted Heath, Rosemary Squires, Ronnie Scott, Humphrey Lyttelton, Terry Dene, Lonnie Donegan, Cleo Laine, Joan Regan, Jimmy Lloyd, Marty Wilde, Tommy Steele and many other members.

SCIF recruited these musicians and other celebrities to be the public face of anti-racism. The logic was simple: teenagers loved rock n roll; they watched shows like *Six-Five Special*; they identified with the stars on the shows, learnt of their membership of SCIF and this would influence their opinions on race. This is not to say that *Six-Five Special* was overtly political – it was not – but the stars from the show were open about their SCIF membership in the weekly music newspapers and organised gigs and fundraisers separate to the show. The intention was to make racism unattractive and unpopular by suggestion. However, one edition screened immediately after the riots contained a film made by SCIF member and hugely popular singer Marty Wilde, which did directly address the violence and the racism of the riots:

> I remember [the] racial problem in our country…my manager Larry Parnes felt that I might help to calm down the situation if I appealed to the younger people to refrain from violence, as my status as a pop star could influence a potentially dangerous situation on our streets. A film was made with me appealing for calm, and for the younger element to cool down.[21]

Six-Five Special stopped broadcasting in early 1959, when producer Jack Good jumped ship from the BBC and went over to ITV to produce a new show *Oh Boy!* but many of its stars and SCIF members went with him. The presenter on *Oh Boy!* was Tony Hall, who was in SCIF. One of the resident performers on the show was Cuddly Dudley, Britain's first black rock n roller and an active SCIF member.

SCIF's recruitment of Frank Sinatra and Paul Robeson was also a reflection of how far reaching its influence was. Following Sinatra's Oscar winning performance in *From Here To Eternity* in 1953 and his new musical relationship with Nelson Riddle, both his film and musical career had undergone a renaissance that established him as one of the world's most famous celebrities. Sinatra's two articles for SCIF therefore had a massive impact. Paul Robeson (who alongside Claudia Jones was another victim of senator Joseph McCarthy's witch-hunts) was residing in Britain in 1958. Robeson, a Shakespearean actor and singer was arguably the world's most popular African-American artist. Robeson played a part in a variety of SCIF activities. Their level of fame ensured their contributions to SCIF carried a weight far greater than SCIF's diminutive size.

The first to issue a statement opposing the racism of the riots, the first to become politically active against that racism, the first to organise social events opposing the colour-bar, SCIF had – inside a matter of months – launched Britain's only high profile campaign against racism. Their campaign had seen it recruit world celebrities. It had seen the BBC beam the SCIF Christmas party into homes all over the country. Every Saturday night millions of young people watched SCIF singers, actors and comedians on prime time music programmes. Within six months of the riots SCIF was in every living room advocating an anti-fascist and anti-racist opposition to the WDL and Mosley on *Panorama*. No other organisation anywhere in the country, be it political or cultural, had managed to obtain the platform opposing violence and racism that SCIF achieved.

Notes

1   Although promised this event did not happen.

2   *http://www.rulit.me/books/interesting-times-a-twentieth-century-life-read-233799-68.html*

3   Ibid.

4   He polled just 479 votes out of 6,500 cast.

5   Sherwood p70.

6   Smith (2008) p462.

7   Smith (2008) p463.

8   All quotes: The *Kensington Post*, 14 March 1958.

9   Foot (1964) p224.

10   Glass (1960) p198.

11   *http://www.camdennewjournal.com/feature-books-how-change-world-tales-marx-and-marxism-eric-hobsbawm*

12   Hobsbawm, (1998) p178.

13   *Melody Maker*, 28 March 1959.

14   These 'characteristics' were the racist stereotypes we are now very familiar with: propensity to violence, over-sexed, preponderance of disease, laziness, drug taking and uncleanliness, etc etc,. *https://www.youtube.com/watch?v=oVcWVjNOCFA*

15   *https://www.youtube.com/watch?v=oljI2PMUfwY*

16   Ibid.

17   Ibid.

18   Ibid.

19   Ibid.

20   *http://www.screenonline.org.uk/tv/id/1321302/*

21   Interview with Marty Wilde 16/12/16.

08: Lonely Teardrops

AFTER THE RIOTS, as they had done in the 1930s and 1940s, the fascists coalesced. Historically, an increase in fascist activity had always meant an escalation in anti-Semitic attacks. Throughout the summer of 1959 there were reports of increased violence against black people and another shooting. On 17 May a 32 year old carpenter Kelso Cochrane, from Antigua, was walking home from hospital, his arm in a sling, when he was set upon by a gang of white youths. Cochrane was fatally stabbed during the incident. Eye witnesses said they heard repeated racist abuse directed at Cochrane. Though he had no money on him the police insisted it was a robbery and no racial motive existed. For black people people in North Kensington a sense of déjà vu prevailed. As we have seen, Scotland Yard had gone to great lengths to refute racism as a cause of the 1958 riots: 'There had not really been a racial element...but was the work of ruffians, both coloured and white hell-bent on hooliganism'.[1]

Thousands of people, black and white, lined the route of Cochrane's funeral to show respect. The denial of racism in his murder on top of the efforts of the police to deny any prejudice in the previous summer's riots was a defining moment in post-war British history and sullied relations between the black community and the Metropolitan police for decades to follow. It is arguable whether they ever recovered. Years later Peter Dawson, a Union Movement member at the time, admitted it was one of Mosley's party that had killed Cochrane in a racially motivated attack.

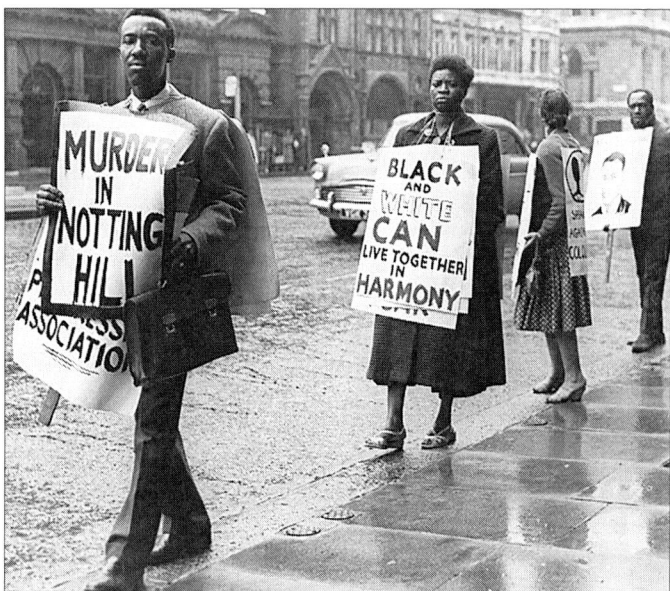

Kelso Cochrane, a black immigrant from Antigua, was stabbed to death by a white youth in Notting Hill in 1959. It was greeted with outrage among the Black community, some of whom marched down Whitehall holding protest banners to highlight the case in Whitehall amid allegations of a police coverup.

Immediately following the death of Cochrane, SCIF issued another publication again called *What The Stars Say*, 'which they [were] distributing in the Notting Hill area to counteract the flood of propaganda being issued there by the racialist bodies'.[2] The lead article was an anti-racist polemic written by Frank Sinatra specifically for SCIF, entitled 'You Can't Hate And Be Happy.' On the front page an entreaty called:

> Very urgently on all men and women who respect their fellow human creatures, uncompromisingly to denounce all instances of racial intolerance they may meet with... That every man and woman living in our country shall be judged entirely by his or her personal qualities and not by the racial group into which each of us happens to be born.[3]

Making their own personal and political point, black women Cleo Laine and Lena Horne appeared in photographs with their white husbands, Johnny Dankworth and Lennie Hayton, happy together and defiant, in clear opposition to Mosley's call for a prohibition on mixed marriages. In another article the broadsheet carried information from:

> An international panel of scientists appointed by the United Nations which has found that racial discrimination has no scientific foundation in biological fact and that the range of mental capacities in all races is the same.[4]

Other contributions came from Lonnie Donegan who said: 'The worst kind of bigotry of all is racial prejudice'.[5] Fellow SCIF member Tommy Steele declared: 'Louis Armstrong, Count Basie, Duke Ellington, Paul Robeson, Joe Louis... show me better whites than these'.[6] Folk singer and SCIF founding member Karl Dallas explained to this writer that:

> We recruited Lonnie and Tommy as we knew the Teddy Boys listened to them and rock n roll came from black America so we thought we could challenge the racism by using the stars they liked.[7]

In counteracting the racism of the WDL and the UM, SCIF were becoming politically sophisticated. They employed a combination of methods to undermine the racist arguments they faced. The populism of teenage celebrity (Donegan and Steele) to send a message to young people; Laurence Olivier and Paul Robeson to add a 'cultured' thespian credibility to their anti-racist cause; physical evidence that racially mixed marriages do work using Cleo Laine and Lena Horne and their white husbands. An international perspective was given from a world superstar Frank Sinatra; and empirical facts were presented by scientists to reject the racial superiority theories from the fascists. This broadsheet was posted through local letter boxes, handed out in the streets and clubs of Notting Hill, Soho and the West End of London.

For Colin Jordan and the WDL Cochrane's death was proof that the 'evils of the coloured invasion' will only lead to trouble. That fascists were responsible for this tragedy he overlooked.[8] Their activities continued in and around the area. Immediately after the murder, Mosley held several highly provocative Union Movement meetings on the exact spot where Cochrane was slain. A general election had been called for October 1959 with Mosley standing in the North Kensington ward. Determined to capitalise on the tragic death of a young black man and the antagonisms of white people toward the black community, Mosley used all the experience he had gathered in the 1930s and 1940s to gain political traction from racial unease. He situated his campaign office in Kensington Park Road, opposite the local synagogue, which subsequently became regularly daubed with swastikas. For a small organisation the sheer scale of the campaign is impressive. There was an enormous effort involving hundreds of meetings, indoor and out, demonstrations, marches, leafleting, paper sales and sustained canvassing. Mosley's campaign, called by some at the time 'the ugly election', was dripping with racism. Mosley repeatedly announced he was in Notting Hill 'to call a spade a spade'.[9] Insinuations that black people were uncivilised and ate cat food were commonplace and at his street corner meetings Mosley used the local Teddy Boy 'joke', 'Lassie for dogs Kit-e-Kat for wogs'.[10] In his memoir Trevor Grundy recalled Mosley:

> Shouting, ranting and raving that West Indian men captured English girls and kept them locked up in flats, where the girls were repeatedly raped.[11]

Despite the intense activity, the outcome from the election was disappointing for the fascists: the UM lost their deposit. Mosley polled only 8.1% with 2,811 votes. This was his penultimate crusade before he finally admitted defeat after faring even worse in the 1966 election and scurried off to France for the remainder of his life. Colin Jordan became the leader – or to call him by his official sobriquet 'World Führer '– of the paradoxically named World Organisation of National Socialists.[12] He was involved in an increasingly bizarre collection of openly Nazi groups until he lost what credibility he had in fascist circles when he was arrested for stealing three pairs of red women's knickers from Tesco's in Leamington Spa in 1975.

SCIF were a reactive anti-racist organisation. Whilst racism certainly did not go away after Mosley's defeat in 1959, the fascist parties that fed off of that racism were undermined by the response to Kelso Cochrane's death and the thousands of hours of work put in to counteract their racism by SCIF and many other organisations and individuals. With the UM and WDL in retreat, SCIF's raison d'être diminished. 'SCIF was a short lived thing that didn't really become a campaign as such, it just ran its course', recalled founding member Hylda Sims.[13] The last mention I could find of SCIF was a small advert for a gig in South East London, tucked away in the corner of page seven in *Melody Maker* on 14 November 1959, entitled 'Jazz stars to play for SCIF funds':

> A jazz ball in aid of the Stars Campaign for Interracial Friendship will be held at Dulwich Baths on 14 December. Giving their services free will be Johnny Dankworth, The Lennie Best Quartet, Norman Days Jazzmen, Kenny Robinson's Jazz Band and blues singer guitarist Alex Korner.[14]

For the jazz and blues world the importance nee reverence of black musicians had always informed their politics.[15] In pop music and rock n roll this corollary was sometimes not there, as audiences in the UK often heard black American songs for the first time through white performers doing cover versions, making this black to white link 'once removed'. The first mass sub-culture for British teenagers was the Teddy Boy and although it adopted a musical expression, it was primarily a social manifestation of alienation, dissatisfaction and post-war hangover. By 1960 it was beginning to wane, certainly in London, and in its place a new sub-culture was forming. Modernists, who SCIF member Colin MacInnes discusses so eloquently in *Absolute Beginners*, were not the same as the Teddy Boys. Like MacInnes, they celebrated black culture, they lived black culture. They shared the same clothes, the same clubs, the same drugs and the same music as their West Indian neighbours.[16]

Part of the job that was done by SCIF in its short life – championing black culture – was taken up by a new set of teenagers, mods in London. It was also passionately promoted by a new wave of musicians in the 1960s with an incomparable fanbase to that of the jazz and skiffle players in SCIF. The Beatles, The Rolling Stones, The Kinks, The Animals, et al, all were blues and RnB fanatics, constantly name checking the black sources of their inspiration and bringing black American artists over to the UK to tour with them in large arenas.

Most importantly an organised black British response to racism had been awoken, and would never return to slumber. There was also much that had happened during this time in the wider world to challenge at least some of the racist misconceptions that the '58 generation had ingested. The Sharpeville Massacre in South Africa and the struggle against apartheid, the March on Washington and the ongoing Civil Rights Movement in America, The Algerian war, Aldermaston, Ban the Bomb and The Bay of Pigs crisis. Britain was also slowly coming to terms with its diminishing role as a world player. As SCIF member Eric Hobsbawm outlined in his work *The Age of Empire*, no imperialism or colonial power can last forever. Paradoxically, the war that Britain had fought to save its empire proved to be the catalyst for its demise.

Notes

1   *Kensington Post* 24 September 1958.
2   *The Daily Worker* 27 May 1959. One of the reasons SCIF used free broadsheets to carry their message was in reply to the *North Kensington Leader*, a fascist broadsheet circulated by Mosley's Union Movement around the Notting Hill area.
3   Ibid.
4   Ibid.
5   *Melody Maker* 28 May 1958.
6   Ibid.
7   Telephone interview Karl Dallas 06/07/2015.
8   *https://www.youtube.com/watch?v=JlYgCpA6z2M*
9   Grundy (1999) p180.
10 Ibid. Lassie was a brand of dog food popular at the time Kit-e-Kat was a popular cat food.
11 ibid.
12 Seriously, this was his title. However, on a more sober note Jordan was very influential in the education of John Tyndall and Martin Webster, both of whom became leaders of the National Front and/or the British National Party from the 1960s onwards.
13 Hylda Sims Telephone Interview: 02/09/2015.
14 *Melody Maker* 12 November 1959.
15 Of course there are always exceptions to the rule as evidenced by Eric Clapton's racist tirade in Birmingham in 1976 supporting Enoch Powell's 'Rivers of Blood' speech.
16 I would argue here that there are in fact three phases of Mod: 1: The Modernists that MacInnes talks about, lovers of jazz and Ivy League clothing from 1957-1960. 2: The R&B Mods of Soho clubs like the Scene and the Flamingo wearing Italian clothes 1960-1963. 3: The Fred Perry & Levi mods, lovers of The Who and Small Faces and Brighton scooter runs 1963-1965.

09: A Change is Gonna Come

WHAT WERE THE results of the tumultuous events of 1958 and 1959 and what did SCIF achieve? For hagiographers the world is often explained through single events, the great battles or key moments in an epoch where monumental and catalysmic decisions are made by men of valour. For the historian interested in social history the world is more complicated, opaque and certainly less didactic. No single event, person or organisation can be held solely responsible for the 1958 riots or the amelioration that would slowly develop in the decades following them. Mao Zedong once remarked 'the longest journey starts with the smallest step'. Indeed, the journey that began in Notting Hill has yet to reach its destination. However, much that has been achieved since has its origins in the events in west London that summer of 1958. The myriad organisations that were born to fight discrimination and oppression in the late 1950s pushed anti-racism onto the political agenda. Although Britain had to wait a further seven years until legislation was passed that sought to address the systematic inequality of black people, the first fledgling delegations to parliament seeking to enable such legislation came from the smoking remnants of Notting Hill.

SCIF sought to use the celebrity of its members to make anti-racism respectable – even cool – in 1950s Britain. That some of its members were journalists in the music press ensured that in the year after the riots SCIF was never far from the news. Denis Preston, Fred Dallas, Max Jones and Humphrey Lyttelton all used their columns in the *Melody Maker* and the *New Musical Express* to promote anti-racist events and argue a political line out of step with large parts of society. For a small organisation SCIF punched well above its weight.

The most obvious legacy of SCIF and the 1958 riots is the Notting Hill Carnival. Many later on claimed parental rights of Carnival but the correlation between the inaugural – albeit indoor – carnival in St Pancras Town Hall and the North Kensington troubles seems irrefutable. Claudia Jones, one of SCIFs leading members and a Trinidadian by birth, saw through her involvement with SCIF the power of music and its potential to disarm racist ideas. That the first Carnival is held just five months after the riots in January 1959 and Jones's statement that with Carnival we 'wash the taste of Notting Hill and Nottingham out of our mouths' combined with her nom-de plume as 'the mother of carnival' all suggest that the festival is her baby.[1]

The year after Claudia Jones's death, the Race Relations Act of 1965 made racial prejudice illegal and forbade discrimination on the 'grounds of colour, race, or ethnic or national origins' in public places. The bill had lost its teeth as it made its way through the parliamentary process and when passed into law, racial discrimination was watered down to a civil offence rather than a criminal one. Furthermore, the law did not apply to discrimination in employment, housing or shops. The key areas of concern for black people were: the ability to secure gainful employment; to receive equal pay to their white counterparts for such employment; to have somewhere safe, clean and affordable to live; and an end to the colour bar in shops, restaurants and pubs. The 1965 Act did nothing to enshrine such concepts in criminal law. Nevertheless, this was progress. As an adjunct, a Race Relations Board was set up to oversee any problems in the future, and problems there were.

Harold Macmillan's government sought to address concerns over immigration by introducing a bill that inhibited it. The 1962 Commonwealth Immigration Act restricted immigration from black or Asian countries. No longer would a British passport guarantee residence in the UK. This act legitimised discrimination toward potential migrants of colour and was to be the bedrock for future legislation passed by Labour and Conservative alike: Wilson's 1968 New Commonwealth Act; Heath's 1971 Immigration Act and many more over the next forty years. The 1964 election saw Conservative candidate Peter Griffiths campaigning in the Smethwick constituency in the West Midlands on the slogan 'If you want a nigger for a neighbour, vote Labour'. He won with a seven percent swing.

By 1968 Conservative ex-health minister Enoch Powell had developed political schizophrenia and was disagreeing with himself over the very immigrants he had travelled to the four corners of the commonwealth to recruit just ten years prior. He was now demanding repatriation. That same year, a dockers' strike and subsequent demonstrations in support of Powell's infamous 'Rivers of Blood' speech were combined with numerous violent attacks on black people up and down the country. They were a chilling reminder of 1958 and an indication that the so-called Summer of Love in 1967 had not shined much further than the Circle Line on the London Underground. However, all these events were, to a degree, tempered by a resistance that had begun in 1958.

Sixteen years after significant immigration began, the Home Secretary Rab Butler finally established the Commonwealth Immigrants Advisory Council in 1964 which looked into the issues faced by immigrants in their local areas. The Campaign Against Racial Discrimination was also founded that year to lobby the new Labour government for anti-discrimination laws. Further legislation was passed amending the 1965 Act. The Race Relations Act 1968 (which ironically fuelled Powell's tirade) finally made it illegal to refuse housing, employment, or public services to a person on the grounds of colour, race, ethnic or national origins. It also created the Community Relations Commission to promote 'harmonious community relations'. This act would be amended in 1976, in 2000 and again in 2010, each modification improving on the initial legislation. The baton of oppression too was passed from the beleaguered Afro-Caribbean community to the newly arriving Kenyan and Ugandan Asians fleeing persecution in Africa, as they received the brunt of racist bile from the intolerant and un-accommodating. This new influx of immigrants and the hostility against them revived the fortunes of the latest incarnation of neo-Nazis, the National Front (NF).

The growth in racist and fascist ideas and a worrying increase in violent attacks against black and Asian people saw the creation of Rock Against Racism (RAR) in 1976, a collection of musicians, socialists and enthusiasts organised together to campaign against racial prejudice. It was launched after the racist rant from guitarist Eric Clapton in support of Enoch Powell's 'Rivers of Blood' speech. RAR was a propaganda tool, it used music and the fame of its members to combat far-right and racist ideas. A direct – although unknowing – descendant of SCIF it trod an uncannily similar path, but this time with substantially more success. It saw a succession of massive gigs, most famously 80,000 people assembling in Victoria Park, London in 1978 to see The Clash, Steel Pulse, X-Ray Specs, and the Tom Robinson Band. RAR was instrumental in counter-acting the growth of far-right ideas in Britain at the time. The NF were beating the Liberal Party into third place in elections in the mid-1970s and the combination of RAR, the Anti-Nazi League (ANL) and combined black and Asian organisations ensured their demise by the end of the decade.

The legacy of SCIF lives on in its grandchild, Love Music Hate Racism, (LMHR). Set up in 2002, LMHR was a direct response to the growth of the British National Party (BNP) and again sought to combat racist ideas using the power of music. Many gigs were organised of which Manchester's Platt Fields Park, headlined by Doves and Ms Dynamite in 2002 was a highlight. On 28 April 2008 LMHR organised an anniversary gig in Victoria park to commemorate the RAR gig thirty years before. There has been no such commemoration for SCIF. As I write LMHR is undergoing a rebirth, as levels of xenophobia and racism reach alarming levels in the post Brexit and Trump epoch.

The history of SCIF, RAR and LMHR, I believe, is incomplete and there is more research needed to compare and contrast SCIF with the two organisations that superseded it in later years. The relationship between music and anti-fascism in twentieth century Britain needs its proper place in history. Until now part of that history has been lost. This needs redressing; it must not get lost again. Mindful of this, the last word should go to Ruth Glass, sociologist and author way back in 1959, from her unparalleled study *Newcomers: The West Indians in London*:

> About fifty years from now, future historians – in Asia, in Africa and perhaps in England – writing about Europe in the nineteen fifties and sixties will presumably devote a chapter to the coloured minority group in this country. They will say that although this group was small, it was an important, indeed an essential one. For its arrival and growth gave British society an opportunity of recognising its own blind spots, and also looking beyond its own nose to a widening horizon of human integrity. They will point out that the relations between white and coloured people in this country were a test of Britain's ability to fulfil the demands for progressive rationality in social organisation, so urgently imposed in the latter part of the twentieth century. And the future historians will add that Britain had every chance of passing this test, because at that period her domestic problems were rather slight by comparison to those of many other areas of the world. All this can be anticipated. But it is still uncertain how the chapter will end.[2]

Notes

1   Sherwood (1999) p89.
2   Glass (1960) p237.

Discography of chapter titles

Forty Miles of Bad Road — **Duane Eddy: London** 1959. Was a rock and roll instrumental single recorded by Duane Eddy. It charted #9. It also appeared on Eddy's 1960 album $1,000,000 Worth of Twang.

High Hopes — **Frank Sinatra: Capitol Records** 1959. High Hopes was recorded by Frank Sinatra in 1959 in a hit version. The track peaked at #6 in the UK Singles Chart. Frank Sinatra recorded a version of the tune with different lyrics which was used as the theme song for the 1960 presidential campaign of John Kennedy.

London Is The Place For Me — **Lord Kitchener: Juno Records** 1948. When the *Empire Windrush* arrived at Tilbury on 21 June 1948, and inaugurated modern Caribbean immigration to Britain, it also supplied calypso with its best known image, on *Pathe* newsreel, Lord Kitchener singing his new composition *London Is The Place For Me.*

Rock With The Caveman — **Tommy Steele: Decca Records** 1956. Tommy Steele had a hit with this song and he is often described as Britain's first Rock n Roller. He was an early member of SCIF.

On The Street Where You Live — **Vic Damone: Columbia Records** 1956. Originally from the musical *My Fair Lady*, which opened in 1956. The most popular version of the song was recorded by Vic Damone in 1956 for Columbia Records. It was a No.1 hit in the UK Singles Chart in 1958.

Great Balls Of Fire — **Jerry Lee Lewis: Sun Records** 1957. Written by Otis Blackwell and Jack Hammer the song featured in the 1957 movie *Jamboree* and was a top ten hit for Lewis in the UK in 1958. The less said about Jerry Lee Lewis's life and politics, the better.

Smoke Gets In Your Eyes — **The Platters: Mercury Records** 1958. Originally written in 1933 for a musical *Roberta*, the most well-known version of Smoke Gets in Your Eyes was recorded by The Platters. The group's cover became a number one hit in the US, on the Billboard Hot 100 music chart in 1959. On the UK charts the song spent five weeks at the top during February and March of that same year.

What a Diff'rence a Day Makes — **Dinah Washington: Mercury Records** 1959. A song originally written in Spanish Cuando vuelva a tu lado (When I Return to Your Side) by María Grever, a Mexican songwriter, in 1934. Dinah Washington's version was top ten in the UK in 1959.

Lonely Teardrops — **Jackie Wilson: Brunswick Records** 1958. Partly written and produced by Berry Gordy, this song is considered by the Rock'n roll hall of fame as one of the most influential in twentieth century musical history. It was an R&B number one in the States.

A Change is Gonna Come — **Sam Cooke: RCA Victor Records** 1963. The song contains the refrain, 'It's been a long time coming, but I know a change is gonna come.' It was inspired by various personal experiences in Cooke's life, most prominently an event in which he and his entourage were turned away from a whites only motel in Louisiana. It was released as a single after his death in 1964.

SCIF Members

Larry Adler An American musician, one of the world's most skilled harmonica players.

Eamonn Andrews An Irish radio and television presenter who worked in Britain.

Winifred Atwell A Trinidadian pianist who enjoyed great popularity in Britain and Australia.

Chris Barber British jazz musician, best known as a bandleader and trombonist.

Long John Baldry An English blues singer and a voice actor.

Max Bygraves An English comedian, singer, actor and variety performer.

Pearl Carr An English entertainer, singer, part of duo with Teddy Johnson (see below).

Alma Cogan An English singer of pop music.

Ken Colyer An English jazz trumpeter and cornetist, devoted to New Orleans jazz.

Edric Connor A pioneering Caribbean singer, folklorist and actor.

Fred Dallas A British journalist, musician, author, playwright, peace campaigner, record producer and broadcaster.

Johnny Dankworth An English jazz composer, saxophonist and clarinetist.

Lonnie Donegan A Scottish singer, songwriter and musician, referred to as the King of Skiffle, who influenced 1960s British pop musicians.

Charlie Drake An English comedian, actor, writer and singer.

Ray Ellington Popular English singer and bandleader.

Tony Hancock	An English comedian and actor.
Richard Hauser	An Austrian Quaker sociologist and social commentator.
Tubby Hayes	An English jazz multi-instrumentalist, best known for his tenor saxophone playing.
Ted Heath	A British musician and big band leader.
'Cuddly' Dudley Heslop	An English rock & roll singer, and actor, who came to fame on the *Oh Boy!* TV series, and is noted for being Britain's first black rock & roller.
Eric Hobsbawm	A British Marxist historian and member of Communist Party.
Frank Holder	A Guyanese jazz singer and percussionist .
Teddy Johnson	An English singer and entertainer – other half of Pearl Carr.
Max Jones	Music critic, jazz enthusiast, activist.
Claudia Jones	A Trinidadian political activist and campaigner.
Cleo Laine	An English jazz and pop singer and an actress.
Humphrey Lyttelton	An English jazz musician and broadcaster.
Bert Lloyd	An English folk singer and collector of folk song.
Ewan MacColl	A Scottish folk singer, songwriter, communist, labour activist, actor, poet, playwright and record producer.
Colin MacInnes	An English novelist.
George Melly	An English jazz and blues singer, critic, writer and lecturer.
Hephzibah Menuhin	An American/Australian pianist, writer, and human rights campaigner.
Matt Monro	An English ballad singer.
Pete Murray	A British radio and television presenter and a stage and screen actor.

Mick Mulligan	An English jazz trumpeter and bandleader.
Laurence Olivier	An English actor.
Ottilie Patterson	A Northern Irish blues singer best known for her performances and recordings with the Chris Barber Jazz Band.
Denis Preston	A British record producer and music critic.
Russell Quaye	An English musician and promoter.
Marion Ryan	A popular British singer.
Ronnie Scott	An English jazz tenor saxophonist and jazz club owner.
Harry Seacombe	A Welsh comedian and singer.
Peter Sellers	A British film actor, comedian and singer.
Tommy Steele	An English entertainer, regarded as Britain's first teen idol and rock and roll star.
Eric Sykes	An English radio, television and film writer, actor and director.
Hylda Sims	An English musician and poet.
Dickie Valentine	An English pop singer and entertainer.
Frankie Vaughan	An English singer of Easy Listening and pop music.
Kent Walton	A British television sports commentator and presenter.
Marty Wilde	An English singer and songwriter.
David Whitfield	A popular British male tenor vocalist.

Musical movements

Tropicália also known as Tropicalismo, is a Brazilian artistic movement that arose in the late 1960s. It encompassed art forms such as theatre, poetry, and music. A combination of the popular and the avant-garde, as well as a fusion of traditional Brazilian culture with foreign influences characterized the movement.

The Nova Cançó (Meaning in English "The New Song") was an artistic movement that promoted Catalan music in Franco's Spain. The movement sought to normalise use of the Catalan language in popular music and denounced the injustices of the Franco regime. The Group de Folk, which emerged in the same period, also promoted a new form of popular music in Catalan, drawing inspiration from contemporary American and British music. Many defied such repression and underground clubs existed where Germans performed and listened to jazz, at the peril of their liberty, or worse.

Jazz in Nazi Germany After a sustained campaign, Reich Minister for Propaganda Joseph Goebbels banned jazz music in Nazi Germany in 1935. This forced listeners underground. The more serious jazz listeners in Germany went to illegal clubs to listen to their music. There were also the Swing kids. They were a movement of young people who dressed, danced, and listened to jazz in defiance of the Nazi regime. The Nazi Party acted against this movement by detaining several of the young leaders of the Swing Youth and sending them to concentration camps.

Further Information

For anyone interested in this era, and wanting some further information. The following is a series of top ten recommendations for your listening, watching and reading pleasure. Not all were made in 1958/9 or are necessarily about Notting Hill, but they all give a flavour of the period.

BRITISH SKIFFLE TOP 10: (compiled by Billy Bragg)

Rock Island Line — Lonnie Donegan
Freight Train — Chas McDevitt with Nancy Whiskey
Don't You Rock Me Daddy-O — The Vipers
Last Train to San Fernando — Johnny Duncan
Can't You Line 'Em — Chris Barber's Skiffle Group
Midnight Special — The City Ramblers
Take This Hammer — Ken Colyer
Mama Don't Allow — Les Hobeaux
Death Letter — Alexis Korner Skiffle Group
Raise A Ruckus Tonight — Eden Street Skiffle Group

BRITISH MODERN JAZZ TOP 10: (compiled by Tony Higgins)

Playtime — Don Rendall
Blue Bogey — Wilton Gaynair
The Couriers of Jazz — Jazz Couriers
In Concert — Jazz Couriers
Pal Jimmy — Jimmy Deucher
The Five Of Us — Jazz Five
London Jazz Quartet — Tubby Hayes
Tubby's Groove — Tubby Hayes
London Jazz Quartet — London Jazz Quartet
Blues In Trinity — Dizzy Reece

BRITISH ROCK 'N' ROLL TOP 10: (compiled by Mitch Mitchell)

Please Don't Touch — Johnny Kidd & The Pirates
Shakin All Over — Johnny Kidd & The Pirates
Sweet Little Sixteen — Michael Cox

Czardas — Nero & The Gladiators
Don't You Just Know It — Lord Sutch
Jezebel — Marty Wilde
Gonna Type A Letter To You — Billy Fury
Teen Scene — The Hunters
Tribute To Buddy Holly — Mike Berry
Big Fat Mama — Roy Young

BRITISH LITERATURE TOP 10: (compiled by Jason Brummell)

Absolute Beginners — Colin MacInnes
City of Spades — Colin MacInnes
Mr Love & Justice — Colin MacInnes
Lonely Londoners — Sam Selvon
A Taste Of Honey — Shelagh Delaney
Paid Servant — E R Braithwaite
To Sir, With Love — E R Braithwate
Saturday Night and Sunday Morning — Alan Sillitoe
The Loneliness of the Long Distance Runner — Alan Sillitoe
This Sporting Life — David Storey

BRITISH FILM TOP 10: (compiled by Rick Blackman)

The Wind Of Change — Directed by Vernon Sewell
Sapphire — Directed by Basil Dearden
A Taste Of Honey — Directed By Tony Richardson
West 11 — Directed by Michael Winner
Saturday Night and Sunday Morning — Directed by Karel Reisz
A Kind of Loving — Directed by John Schlesinger
Look Back in Anger — Directed by Tony Richardson
Violent Playground — Directed by Basil Dearden
Room At The Top — Directed by Jack Clayton
Billy Liar — Directed by John Schlesinger

Bibliography

Beckman, Morris (1993), *The 43 Group*, Centreprise Publications, London

Bennett, Tony (1993) *Rock and Popular Music: Politics, Policies, Institutions*, Routledge, London

Boggs, Carl *(1978) Gramsci's Marxism*, Pluto Press, London

Braun, Aurel (1997) *The Extreme Right*, Westview press, London

Cronin, Mike (1996) *The Failure of British Fascism*, Macmillan, London

Callinicos, Alex (1987) *The Revolutionary Ideas of Karl Marx*, Bookmarks, London

Cohen, Sara (1993) *Ethnography and Popular Music Studies*, Cambridge University Press, Cambridge

Cohen, Stanley (2009) *Folk Devils and Moral Panics, The Creation of the Mods and Rockers*, Routledge, London

Denselow, Robin (1989) *When the Music's Over: The Story of Political Pop*, Faber and Faber, London

Eatwell, Roger (2014) *The New Extremism in 21st Century Britain*, Routledge, London

Eatwell, Roger (2008) *Fascism and the Extreme Right*, Routledge, London

Foot, Paul (1965) *Immigration and Race in British Politics*, Penguin, Harmondsworth

Fryer, Paul, (2010) *Staying Power, The History of Black People in Britain*, Pluto Press, London

Glass, Ruth (1960) *Newcomers The West Indians in London*, Centre for Urban Studies, University College Press, London

Gould, Tony (1986) *Inside Outsider, The Life & Times of Colin MacInnes*, Penguin, Harmondsworth

Griffin, Roger (1995) *Fascism*, Oxford University Press, USA

Griffin, Roger (1993) *The Nature of Fascism*, Routledge, London

Griffin, Roger (2008) *A Fascist Century*, Palgrave Macmillan, Basingstoke

Griffin, Roger (2007) *Modernism and Fascism*, Palgrave Macmillan, Basingstoke

Griffin, Roger (2003) *International Fascism: Theories, Causes and the New Consensus* Oxford University Press, USA

Grundy, Trevor (1999) *Memoirs of A Fascist Childhood*, Arrow Books, London

Hebdige, Dick (2009) *Subculture, The Meaning of Style*, Routledge, London

Hobsbawm, E J (1989) *The Jazz Scene*, Weidenfeld and Nicholson, London

Hobsbawm, E J (1998) *Uncommon People, Resistance, Rebellion and Jazz*, Abacus, London

Hoggart, Richard (1992) *The Uses of Literacy*, Penguin Group, London

Knight, Peter (2002) *Small Scale Research*, Sage, London,

Leach, Robert, (2006) *Theatre Workshop, Joan Littlewood and the Making of Modern British Theatre*, University of Exeter Press, Gateshead

Longhurst, Brian (2009) *Popular Music & Society*, Polity, Cambridge

MacInnes, Colin (1994) *Absolute Beginners*, Penguin, London

MacInnes, Colin (1968) *City of Spades*, Penguin, London

MacInnes, Colin, (1997) *Mr Love & Justice*, Penguin, London

Marx, Karl & Engels, Fredrick (1988) *The Communist Manifesto*, Foreign Language Press, Beijing

Paxton O, Robert (2004) *The Anatomy of Fascism*, Penguin, Harmondsworth

Selvon, Sam (2006) *Lonely Londoners*, Penguin, London

Sherwood, Marika (1999) *Claudia Jones, A Life in Exile*, Lawrence & Wishart, London

Shuker, Roy (2005) *Popular Music The Key Concepts*, Routledge, Abingdon

Smith, Evan (2008) *Class before Race: British Communism and the Place of Empire in Postwar Race Relations*, Guilford Press, London

Street, John (1986) *Rebel Rock: The Politics of Popular Music*. Basil Blackwell, Oxford

Tagg, Phillip (1999) *Introductory Notes to the Semiotics of Music*, photocopied document, Liverpool Hope University.

Thurlow, Richard (2009) *Fascism in Britain, I B Tauris & Co*, London

Trotsky, Leon (1972) *Fascism, What It Is & How to Fight It*, Pathfinder, New York

Vague, Tom (2003) *Getting it Straight in Notting Hill Gate: A West London Psycho-geography* Report, Kindle, London

Van Maanen, John (1988) *Tales Of The Field*, University of Chicago, London

Websites

http://www.netlibrary.net/articles/India_in_World_War_II

http://dictionary.reference.com/browse/politics?s=t

http://www.telegraph.co.uk/news/uknews/terrorism-in-the-uk/10859770/911-terror-attacks-fuelled-decade-long-rise-in-racism-in-the-UK.html

http://www.bbc.co.uk/news/uk-31140919

(http://booth.lse.ac.uk/static/a/4.html)

http://edwardianteddyboy.com

(https://www.youtube.com/watch?v=oljI2PMUfwY)

https://www.youtube.com/watch?v=pFLQkC4ObXc

https://m.youtube.com/watch?v=1PsNmTB4LEA

https://m.youtube.com/watch?v=LnouhBSCnZM

http://www.rulit.me/books/interesting-times-a-twentieth-century-life-read-233799-68.html

● Sixty-seven writers and photographers bring alive the history of a cultural and political movement that helped change the world we live in. Told by participants, unified in a struggle on the dance floor and in the streets, to stop the Nazi National Front and to fight the poison of racism, this book marks RAR's 40th birthday.

● Every generation has to find a way to confront the racists in their midst. This is the story of how we fought them in the 1970's, with our music, art, photography and writing. Inspirational stuff. — **Billy Bragg**

● *Reminiscences of RAR* documents extraordinary stories of activism and heroism, told by everyday people, who challenged the social and political fabric of British life. The battles fought under the banner of Rock Against Racism – gender, race, class – laid the paving stones for future generations to walk upon. An awe-inspiring love letter to the alliance between culture, compassion and street politics. — **Daniel Rachel** (author of *Walls Come Tumbling Down: the music and politics of Rock Against Racism, 2 Tone and Red Wedge*)

£15
ISBN: 978-1910-885-36-9

REMINISCENCES OF RAR

Rocking Against Racism 1976-1982

★ Edited by Roger Huddle & Red Saunders

Available from Bookmarks
https://bookmarksbookshop.co.uk

REDWORDS